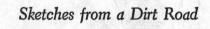

Sketches from a Dirt Road

Sketches from a Dirt Road

GREGORY JAYNES

Illustrations by Richard Cuffari

DOUBLEDAY & COMPANY, INC.
Garden City, New York   1977

Some of the material in this book has appeared in *New Times* and the Atlanta *Constitution*.

"Trapper" was initially published in *Sports Illustrated* under the title "Trappin' Kind of Stands Alone."

"The Ballad of Lamar Fountain" appears courtesy of Walter Gaskins.

Library of Congress Cataloging in Publication Data

Jaynes, Gregory.
  Sketches from a dirt road.

  1. White Co., Ga.—Social life and customs. 2. Jaynes, Gregory. 3. White Co., Ga.—Biography. I. Title.
F292.W48J39   309.1'758'27704
ISBN: 0-385-11505-9
Library of Congress Catalog Card Number: 75-36596

To Leron Daniel Jaynes

"It ain't hard to see why them call 'em pigs."

—HENRY WOODHEAD

Sketches from a Dirt Road

Past

As a boy out of high school I worked on a dredge that kept the channels deep and wide in the Mississippi River. I scraped and painted the dredge from waterline to smokestack. Once a week, I went off in a tug with an ax and a machete and the tug pilot would put me out where the river bluff came closest to a road and I would have to hack out a path from the river through the woods to the road. Just about the moment I had the path cleared, a refrigerated truck would come down the road (it always seemed to me a marvel of logistics) and my next chore would be to tote a week's supply of food for the crew from the truck, down the bluff to the tug, and from the tug to the galley on the second deck of the dredge. And when I wasn't scraping and painting and hauling, I was back on the bluff, using ax and machete to cut a footpath to a beer joint. Wherever we went that summer, from Cairo, Illinois, to Vicksburg, Mississippi, there was always a beer joint at every bend, no matter how far the nearest town. I had to clear the beer joint paths with the thought in mind that a drunken mate would be walking it that evening, and if I left anything in his way, be it stick or stone, he might stumble and fall into the river and drown. I worked alone.

All the members of the crew were more than twice my age and most did not bother to make my acquaintance. I had temporary quarters on the stern above the engines. It was a screened-in room with a bunk bed and a metal footlocker and when it rained and rained hard I unfurled the tarpaulin that hung above the screens. In the night, the water and the sky were black as used motor oil. A hundred-watt bulb in the ceiling above the bunk shed light on *Catcher in the Rye, Lord of the Flies, The Old Man and the Sea, Profiles in Courage, Moby Dick, The Naked and the Dead,* and *Candy.* I particularly liked *Candy.* I read in the night and in the day I worked and whistled and sang all the songs I knew to that time. In the fall I quit the job.

I found work making window jambs. Actually, the jambs were already made; my job was to flock the springs for them. I was a jamb-spring flocker. Jamb springs, given some use, tend to squeak. I was responsible for taking the squeak out of the jamb springs. I fastened sixteen springs to a metal rod with sixteen hooks on it, and I dunked all the springs in a vat of flat gray paint. From there, the springs went into the flocker. The flocker was a barrel with a fan in its bottom. The fan sucked cotton lint up from the base of the barrel and the lint stuck to the freshly painted springs. It was a lot like tarring and feathering. When the springs were flocked full, I hung them on a cart and rolled the cart into a walk-in oven. I baked them at 365 degrees for an hour. I did this from midnight until 8 A.M. I worked alone at the rear of a cavernous factory that in the daytime employed two hundred people. In the daytime, I went to college and studied French. This did not work out.

Through nepotism, I got a job putting out a weekly newspaper in Alabama. I was the newspaper's only employee. I bought a camera and took a picture of the new book at the library. I also took a picture of a golfer who had managed, with one stroke, to kill a mockingbird and score a hole in one. If the ball had not hit the bird, the ball would not have dropped into the hole. The golfer calculated the chances of it ever happening again at a trillion to one. I took his picture standing over the cup, a dead bird in his right hand, a golf ball in his left. The sun was at his back and the picture did not come out. Six months after its foal, the newspaper folded.

I thought for a time that I would like to be a mailman. Here was employment with appeal. You work alone in fresh air and when your bag is empty you are done. Sometimes you run across an amorous housewife. I took an exam and was told that I did well, but no one ever called to offer me a position with the U. S. Postal Service. It looked for a while that I was destined to continue parking cars at an airport in Tennessee. I got to drive all the new expensive cars. I was paid in quarters.

With my experience and background, I could think of nothing more logical than going to New York City. I had a two-tone (blue and rust) 1950 Plymouth and I had forty-five dollars. I shared a garret with an unsuccessful actor and I slept on a lawn chair I bought at a five-and-dime. In the days I worked in the mailroom at Decca Records. In the nights I went to dirty movies.

One day Decca Records sent me over to the Sherry-Netherland with a portable record player and a batch of record albums. They were for Ricky Nelson, who was in town to be on the Ed Sullivan Show. Nelson tipped me a five-dollar bill. I thought through the afternoon that I would keep it as a souvenir, but in the evening I spent it on frozen turkey and beef dinners. Decca Records paid me fifty dollars a week. It was not enough to live on. By a sinful and circuitous route, I next found myself working in Arkansas for a woman who edited a newspaper.

I worked for newspapers for ten years. Also in that ten years, I married and my wife and I produced two children: a boy who thinks quickly and speaks slowly, and a girl who has yet to show inclination to do anything other than raise hell. Both appear honest. Some of the newspapers I worked for were dishonest. I worked for one newspaper in a city of considerable size and this was the major newspaper in town and it would not run a photograph of a Kennedy. It would not run a story about a Kennedy unless it was derogatory. On the other hand, it edited out of news stories any information that cast a bad light on Nixon. This was childish, of course. The publisher was in his eighties. He was senile. Now he is dead.

All of my newspaper employers put posturing toads in positions of importance. There was one man who gave me a two-day head-ache. It was his manner to come up with some sort of contro-versial notion and send his people out to prove it. He once had me try to get Dean Rusk to say we ought to put some curbs in the First Amendment. Dean Rusk would not say this. He had me try twice more, then he tried himself, then he wrote a story that im-plied Dean Rusk thought there ought to be some curbs in the First Amendment but would not say so publicly. That was lying. The pressures of this fool's job jammed his neck, so that his head was permanently canted to the left. I do not know if he still car-ries that affliction. I do know that in those days I genuinely ex-pected him to wake one morning lying on his back, his face down in the pillow, dead from asphyxiation.

I don't work on staff for newspapers anymore, nor do I carry all bad memories of that part of my life. My favorite story, in fact, comes from my newspaper years. A dowager from Washington, D.C., came to the city I last worked in to address a local women's organization. The newspaper intended to publish the speaker's photograph, but somehow it got lost. The photograph surfaced three days later, in an advertisement, with the dowager smil-ing her saintly smile from beneath this headline: "Barnesville Woman Pulls the Chain on Lazy Bowels! Was Constipated Seven Years!" The amount of damages asked in the suit she filed set the record for litigation in the Southeast.

For now, I work alone in my living room with my back to the fire. As best I can judge, only my rooster and I are awake so far today. In a moment, I will have to wake the children and my wife, for they have things to do. That done, I plan first to take a walk and then I plan to construct some new steps for the front porch. So I will put this away. I believe it to be a full and truthful answer to the questionnaire that came yesterday from some old classmates, long forgotten, who now seem bent on putting to-gether a reunion.

One last thing: I am again seriously considering becoming a mailman.

Present

The old man no longer hears. I am told if you scream he can hear you, or hear something, if he wants to, but screaming would be disrespectful because he is so very old. It is best to nod, as I did not long ago when he came to my door. He was holding a shotgun, its barrel pointed at my foot.

"You got a yaller dog?"

I nodded, knowing this was serious. He had not stopped at my house in all the months we had lived here. He and his brother, who also does not hear, built this house sixty-five years ago.

"Your dog got a fox head on him?"

I nodded.

"Been after my chickens. Shot at him. Missed. I catch him, I kill him!"

I closed my eyes and gave him a grave, understanding nod.

"I kill him," he said, this time softly. He turned and walked off the porch and down the drive and on down the dirt road that runs by his house and mine. I watched him, a stooped, gray little man in faded overalls, until he had gone around the bend. Then I called up the dog, whose name is Bert. I do not know the dog's genealogy, nor, I suspect, does he. He came running from the pine stand out back of the house. A single white feather was stuck between the teeth on the left of his mouth, and, if it is possible for a dog to look proud, this one looked proud.

I got a rope from the barn and I tied one end to the dog's collar, the other to the trunk of an apple tree near the house. I left the dog tied there and I went into the house to make coffee and to worry the problem. I wished that my wife were here, but she and our son and daughter were away celebrating someone's birthday. This dog-chicken crisis is not the sort I am accustomed to, for my family and I are fresh on the farm.

After much coffee, it struck me to employ the basic condition-response routine. I got one of our chicks from the coop that I built (I built it to be a rabbit hutch; that is the way things have been going) and the chick and I approached Bert the dog. I put the chick on the ground below the apple tree, well within striking distance of the dog, and I backed away. The dog lunged, and I kicked his butt. The dog and the chick and I went through this psychological maneuver for almost an hour. My sympathies were with the dog, though they should have been with the white leghorn, who was under quite a strain.

When my boot had made the dog sore, he stopped going at the chick. To be sure of success, I released the dog from the rope and ran the chicken past him once more. The bird died violently.

I went inside and rang up my neighbor, Mac, a large man who lives over the ridge back of us. He is on our telephone party line. He has lived here for some years, but still he is not used to the party line. To reach one of the parties on your party line, you must dial the last four digits of their number, and then hang up with your fingers. You can feel the buttons vibrating in the cradle of the phone, and that means the number is ringing. When the buttons stop vibrating it means the party has answered. By the time you realize that someone has answered, the someone who has answered usually has said "hello" two or three times, and has impatiently hung up his end. This is what Mac does. It is what he did when I called him about the chicken problem. I dialed again.

The buttons stopped vibrating and I lifted my fingers and I heard Mac say, "Hello-helloooo-GODDAMMIT!-HELL-oh!"

I identified myself and explained the trouble.

"Tell me," Mac said, "that what you gotta do is tie a dead chicken around a dog's neck and leave it a few days. That'll cure him."

I thanked him and went to fetch the chicken corpse from the paper sack that was to have been its coffin. I called up the dog again and, after several assurances that I would not kick him, he came close enough for me to grab him by the collar. I tied the dead bird to the collar with clothesline, making sure that the corpse was around back of the dog's head. Otherwise, I theorized —and thought myself bright for doing so—the dog would lighten his burden by eating it.

The dog grew dotty after a few days. He would come around the house and one or the other of us would say, "Phew! Get that dog away from here!" He began to chase cars, was determined to kill a car, and, in the end, was hit by a car. I took him in and spread him before the hearth and removed the smelly chicken. In two days, the dog was up and about, with a slight limp. Now he chases neither chickens nor cars. However, he is pregnant.

We are living here for all the trite and romantic reasons. We knew nothing of country, but yearned to know it before the state paved it, or the federals claimed it and salted it with concrete picnic tables.

In the city, my children held a higher regard for plastic submarines than for sunny days. My wife, though she had a number of time-consuming interests, found her life metronomic. And I, well, I just wanted to bust out. Let me describe this place:

From the front porch, the view is of a stream, a barn, a black walnut tree, an aging quarter horse, an apple orchard, and a dirt road that snakes over the ridge to the right. Directly across the road, there is a five-acre pasture, and the brown dead stalks of last summer's corn stand there. There is a thicket and another stream just beyond the pasture, and just beyond the stream there is a fifteen-acre pasture, covered with broom sedge at the moment, though we intend to plow it shortly. There is an ailing apple tree in the middle of the larger pasture. Beyond that, there is a mountain called John Jones, and it is thick with poplar, pine, hickory, oak, and sweet gum. Wild dogwoods, too. For the first few days we lived here, I awoke each morning and went outside and hollered, "Vista!" off the front porch. Then the act wore thin, and I stopped.

I doubt that the old brothers who built this house know much of architecture, doubt that they ever heard the word. I know that they cannot read. But their knowledge of simple construction is a knowledge I covet.

They knew, for example, to build a window opposite each window, and a door opposite each door, so the drafts would cool the house in summer. They separated the kitchen from the rest of the house so that the wood stove would not heat the whole place intolerably. They built porches on both sides of the kitchen, and put two doors in that very important room, so that the drafts would save the cook from heat prostration. They built a loftlike second floor, where my children now sleep. The inside walls and ceiling are fashioned of cedar. The brothers knew that termites never touch the stuff, and, besides, it smells good. They built the chimney of fieldstone and mud, and its living-room situation is just so, its draw just right, so that it warms the house nicely in winter. They built a front porch that is two paces wide and a good twenty paces long. The front porch was, and is, the spot most occupied in good weather. And they rested the house on fieldstone piers, all the stones gathered and stacked by the builders.

But now the house is ill from desuetude and the ground has shifted some. The house needs jacking here, shoring there. The main timber beneath the front porch is rotten. Several windowpanes are missing. The tin roof leaks in two spots above the kitchen. A board has worked loose in the living-room floor. We have bees in the wall, snakes in the grass, sparrows in the eaves, and a crude, two-fuse electrical system. I must tend to all this.

I am not good with my hands. A hammer feels odd, a handsaw alien. Just the other day I framed and hung a door, and though it will not close, I am proud of it just the same. It is a step. I will get it to shut. I will borrow a wood plane. I will borrow one tomorrow, or the day after, higgledy-piggledy carpenter, I.

We are living in an area of the Blue Ridge Mountains where people never have had money. I read in the newspapers that repression-depression-oppression is all the worry today. Here it is as it always has been: a man's wealth is measured by the fill of his freezer and the dimensions of his woodpile. We have been here since the spring of 1974, and that, more or less, is what these sketches concern.

Arrival

First night notes:

Bad weary. Everyone asleep—all downstairs, due to bees in wall upstairs. Boy stung a half hour after we got here. He cried, and yelled, "It hurts like crazy!" The girl has refused to go up and look at her bedroom because that is where her brother got tagged with a flying dagger. My wife sleeps, in a bothered fashion, beside me. We argued. We argued because we were exhausted.

God it's dark here. No street lights. No moon. No stars to speak of. Frog noise and katydid noise.

Dinner compliments of the Colonel. A chicken wing, stretched out but uneaten, lies here on the nightstand, a greasy boomerang.

Boxes. Boxes. Boxes. More than this joint will hold. You cannot walk a straight path for the boxes. All to be unloaded. Bees to be gotten rid of. Fear in my children to be gotten rid of. Peace to be made with my wife.

Too beat to account further. Sum: miserable, terribly taxing day. The idyl begins.

Discovery

At breakfast, the boy asked for a BB gun, the girl for a goat. This firearm and this animal, they told me, are absolutely essential to farm life. "What if I'm walking along in the woods," the boy said, "and a bear comes along. What then?" And the girl's reasoning: "I saw a picture of a goat. I like goats." I stalled, saying we could come to terms in the future. They turned up and drank dry their cereal bowls, and set off to explore, the boy convinced that, unarmed, he would be bushwhacked by Cherokees and, being brave, would defend his sister to the death in hand-to-hand combat. "Even if I don't see any Indians," he said, "I'll probably see a rattlesnake and I won't have anything to shoot it with." They left. Babes in the woods.

And so to town to look around, to make known our presence, to pay for services. My wife had to stay home because the stable owner who sold her a quarter horse had promised delivery in the afternoon. She has named the old gelding Mouse because of its color. It sports a single black dorsal stripe. I suspect he is so old that if he had the smarts of the late Trigger, and if you asked him his age, he would begin pawing the ground, and would still be pawing past sundown. "But he's so *gentle*," she says. This horse belongs in a geriatrics barn for the equine.

The woman at the telephone company wanted a twenty-five-dollar deposit, and got it. In the paying, I remembered reading about a whittler in the Ozarks who lives without telephone. "I don't want a bell in my house the whole world can ring!" the whittler said. I told this to the Mercurochrome-haired woman at the phone company. "Ain't it the truth," she said. "Ain't it the truth. I hate the damn thing myself. But I got teen-agers." She put us on a four-party line, the best she had, she said.

On to the electric membership co-operative. We must have electricity for the pump on the well, and for the refrigerator and for the four bare light bulbs that hang from the ceiling in various parts of the house. The clerk wanted a thirty-dollar deposit, and got it. Feeling entirely untrustworthy, I next went to the propane gas dealer.

I bought two hundred gallons of propane gas for fifty-seven dollars and eighty-five cents. This deal was more to my liking. To my mind, utilities have always been mystical. In the city, I was never able to figure the bills. Where did all that natural gas go? How did we use that much electricity? Obviously, the meter is wrong. But the power company holds empirical posture. So I look up ampere and coulomb and ohm and come away confused. Sewage. How does anybody compute sewage? Anyway, I've come to find myself at home with this propane gas dealer. The tank sits out back of the house. (We used to call them Japanese submarines.) The tank holds two hundred gallons. When the gas is gone, the small heater in the living room sputters and goes cold, the stove will not come on, and the pilot light on the water heater spits once and dies. Out of gas. The pipe from the tank leads only to my house. Only I could have expended the whole two hundred gallons. I saw the man pump it in. I see by the meter that now it is empty. I trust this.

At the hardware store, I bought a standard size mailbox, a creosoted pole and a sack of nails. Then I went home and constructed it, and dug a hole out front next to the road, sank it and painted our name in red in capitals along the side. We made the mailbox erection a ceremony, standing back to look at it from this angle and that.

Tuna fish sandwiches and tomato soup for lunch. Flies all in the kitchen. The boy: "I didn't *see* a rattlesnake, but I *heard* one." After lunch, back to the hardware for fly strips, nasty but necessary.

At each stop I asked if anyone were interested in taking a few bees off my hands. I ran into a few beekeepers, all of whom said they were "full up, thank you," and one fine gentleman down the road, who said, "Only keep 'em to pollinate my corn. Tell the truth, I can't stand honey. Stops up my craw."

Driving back, I passed my wife and children, all astride the horse, the horse's head hanging low. "Do you think it's too hot to ride him now?" she said. It was June, but cool, a blue sky day. "No," I said. "Make him rear up, Mom," the boy said. The horse shuffled on off. The biggest pet we've ever had. An eight-hundred-pound dog. A dinosaur.

Now to kill the bees. I went up the stairs, a bug spray in each hand, gunning my way as I ascended. Thousands upon thousands of bees. An entire second story of bees. A carpet of bees. A wall of bees. A ceiling of bees. The air brown with bees. I emptied both aerosol cans before reaching the top stair, and turned, no, ran, well, fell down the stairs, a brown mad cloud in pursuit. To my feet and outside, springing the screen door in the dash. A vengeful few—I'd say a dozen—chased me as far as the drive. We are not being allowed to simply move into this house. We have to storm it, take it, wrest it, bomb it. The birds won, I recall, in Hitchcock's movie.

At the store at the end of the dirt road: ten dollars' worth of Real-Kill. On the way back, my wife and children and a tired old, dun horse have stopped by a creek for water. "Did you get rid of the bees?"

"The war has only begun."

I got the ladder and put it up next to the chimney on the side of the house. I could see the rotted weatherboard where the bees had gained entrance, and only a small crowd hovered outside their

hole to heaven. A skirmish I could win easily, I thought, and then I would fill the entrance with insecticide. If not now, then eventually, this would do the trick. Genocide.

Lying on my back in the hydrangea, having squashed half its beautiful, porcelain white corymbose clusters, having broken its vine by coming quickly to rest upon it from eight feet above, feeling my cheek and forehead beginning to bump out, tiny black darts in the center of each swell, I began to call myself loser. My thought exactly: *You need professional help, ass.*

A viceroy butterfly settled gently on my nose for a moment and said essentially the same thing.

In the evening, détente. The bees controlled the upstairs. None save the suicidal would trespass. They did not descend to our territory. We heard their constant drone, the sound intensity of a Mercury outboard running flat-out in the loft, and I imagined them wing picking a select group of professionals, kamikazes, to finish us off. I tacked a sheet over the entrance to the stairs.

"Dad, can bees kill you?"

"Yes."

"Uh, g'night, Dad."

"Good night. Sleep tight. Don't let the bedbugs bite."

The drone stopped at midnight.

At 2 A.M., the author rose, ice cream on his mind. He made his way in the black toward the kitchen. Just shy of the refrigerator, he made contact with a hanging strip of gook; the strip glommed to the left of his head. Freeing himself, he turned and made his way slowly and carefully back to bed, detaching dead flies from his ear.

The man from Orkin came first thing next day. He had on his back a tank like a tank used by skin divers. He held in his hand a hose with a nozzle. The hose ran from tank to hand. "This'll get 'em," he said. He mounted the ladder. Reaching his target, he got off one shot before being chased to the ground. Back around on the safe side of the house, he said, "Ol' buddy, I don't believe I want to do that again."

"Will that one treatment do it?"

"Nope. We ought to give it a second spray just to make sure."

"Then do it."

"Nope."

"You got to. I'm paying you to."

"I'm gonna do it. I'm gonna do it. One thing I ain't is a chickenshit. Let's just wait till they calm down some."

He drank a beer, taking a long time to finish, and then he climbed the ladder and once more spewed his chemical. Again he was chased down, and he leaped from the fifth rung. He left shaken though uninjured, with thirty-five dollars of our money. In parting, he said, "I'll take termites any day."

We had to call the exterminator back twice more before all the bees died. A different man came each time, and each time, before the second ascent, a beer was consumed, its drinker saying, "I don't make a habit of drinkin' on the job. But this one's a pistol!" Or something like that.

We sucked the little devils up in the Hoover, and I carried the bags to the dump. For weeks, the children anticipated revenge. We all did. We still do.

Mac

We've been eating daily from the vegetable garden and my wife is putting some by. After two unsuccessful plantings, the third try worked and now we have plenty of the usual. List: tomatoes, okra, corn and peas, cucumbers, watermelon, squash, and snap beans. We shared the produce with the McMurtreys (Mac, Betty Jo, Eddie and Alice) and together we worked out an equitable arrangement that made weeding less loathsome. We put the garden in across the road from us, where an apple orchard had lived and died, and we would all go down with buckets and hoes, turn the buckets upside down to sit on, and scoot along the rows, talking as we worked.

Mac, whom I've mentioned before and will mention again, is the head of the McMurtrey tribe. He weighs somewhere in the high two hundreds, shaves his head, looks very much like our idea of Buddha, is a storyteller. It was Mac made the weeding tolerable. Overhead, a gauzy August sun, flies around our heads, our clothes sweat wet, Mac talking, not working, as we move down the rows:

"Feller come by to see me yesterday. Said he's been having headaches. I told him a week or two ago to go see the doctor down in Gainesville. He come by to tell me he'd been to see the doctor and got some tests run on his head. He said to me, 'Mac,' he said, 'that doctor told me I got one thing or another. Told me I either had a tumor in my brain or I got a blood clot in my brain.' "

Mac, his belly beginning to shake: "Doctor didn't leave him much slack, did he?"

Mac was a Marine for twenty-one years and, now that he is out and his children are grown, he sometimes seems to be getting even for all those years he was bossed around. I know that he bosses me, and I take it, because we usually are working in areas in which he is familiar and I am new. More than anything, it was Mac who proved invaluable during our first few weeks of getting used to the country. Mac told us where to dump the garbage, where to get eggs for a dollar a flat, where to get fresh milk and butter. He explained the crude electrical system in the house. He identified birds and insects and snakes for us. My wife told him that she might be interested in raising rabbits and he put her in business (short lived—we found ourselves in possession of the world's only impotent buck).

It was Mac went on a fishing trip in midsummer and returned on a day of swelter to show me what fine eating we were going to have. He opened the trunk lid and putrefaction cold-cocked us. I was sick. His coolers had sprung leaks. His ice had melted, his mackerel decayed.

The pump on the well went out. Just stopped. I took it to Sears in the next town for repairs. Mac and I snaked a pipe all the way from his well to mine, a considerable distance. We rigged it alongside the narrow road that runs over the ridge to his house, being careful to bury it as we went. Near dusk, not long after we had the works connected up and water flowing, a county road grader came along and cut our pipe. The water, forced out by forty pounds of pressure, plus a long downhill run, pooled up three inches deep behind my house before Mac and I could shut it down and repair the cut. We got drunk that night.

Mac once told me, "You gotta make up your mind right off the bat whether you gonna raise your kids or you gonna let some other man's kids raise 'em. A man's gotta get out with his kids, guide 'em, show 'em what he knows. Play with 'em. Otherwise, you lose 'em. They might's well be somebody else's."

And then, after laying that on me, followed it with this: "Now, gasoline is fifty-five-sixty-sixty-five cents a gallon. You see what I mean? [He uses this phrase a lot, to make sure you're paying attention.] My boy Eddie, now you know Eddie. Last night he takes my truck out. It gets to be two o'clock in the morning, three o'clock, four o'clock and I can't sleep. And Eddie ain't in yet. Do you foller me? Five o'clock, hc comes in. I ask him where he's been and he says, 'Out ridin' around.' Out ridin' goddamn around! Gasoline what it is! I liked to killed him! I liked to wrung his neck! Out ridin' around!"

Chickens

My wife put out the word that we were looking for some chickens if anyone wanted to get shed of some. Word came that there were some wild chickens available down the road a few miles, if we were willing to catch them. Now, wild chickens aren't worth eating, unless you want to cook them a week. But they do lay fine eggs.

We got ten paper sacks and headed out. These chickens fly and they roost in trees and they won't sit still until dark. We began the search at gloaming, my son and daughter creeping along with sacks that had CHICKEN crayoned along the sides.

We stumbled through thicket after thicket, each of us covered in burrs and beggar lice, the children continuing to holler, "Here chicken. Here chick-chick-chick-chick-chickeeeeen!" I saw one perched quietly on a stump and I hushed the children and we fanned out figuring to surround her.

She saw me first, and lit out, flying past my ear at twenty miles an hour, sounding like a ten-pound hummingbird. We caught three in the dark that night and returned home, all of us scratched. It was six months before they laid the first egg.

After three eggless months, my wife went round to the poultry place and asked for some culls. She came home with two dozen, only one dozen of which were culls. The chicks that weren't culls were white. They had had shots and they had had their beaks clipped, so they wouldn't hurt one another. The culls were black, and they had received no care, no attention. The man at the poultry place explained that the white chicks peck the black chicks to death so, since there are fewer blacks born than whites, they cull the blacks. Of our twenty-four, twelve lived. Ten of the survivors were black.

Antenna

I am being pressured to purchase and install an antenna for the television. I am reluctant to do so for many reasons, not the least of which is nostalgia. The snowy, fuzzy images we receive on our screen each evening have the same lack of clarity as the set we had when I was young and we were the fourth family in our town to buy a TV. You knew there were people in that blizzard, but you could not make out their features. Hell, most of the time you couldn't make out their sex. As a result of television, I learned the words "audio" and "video" far earlier than I would have in the public educational process. "The network is experiencing difficulty with the visual portion of this program. Please do not adjust your set. We will continue with the audio."

The difference between then and now is that the network is doing fine; the difficulty lies in the placement of our set in a room in a house in a valley ringed by mountains. Which brings me to a second reason I am hedging on this antenna business.

I recall a sad tale from my youth. The first man in our town to buy a television was a friend of my father. He would invite us over on Friday night to watch the Friday Night Fights. We always heard the blow-by-blow, but we saw no grace, no agility, no knock-outs. This pioneer we went to visit was always apologetic. "I'm sorry," he would say, "*really* sorry. You shoulda been here last night. Picture clear as a bell. We stayed up half the night watching everything that came on." To this day, I give the man credit, though just such apologies are the story of my life: "I've never seen the fishing so bad here. We took twenty-seven crappie last time I came"; "I know you paid two hundred dollars for the cottage and it rained every day. Believe me, I'm sorry. Till this week, it ain't rained a drop at the beach all summer"; "No kidding. I ain't ever had a lick of trouble out of this outboard motor. Till today." But back to the fellow who bought the first TV. It infuriated him that reception was so poor on evenings when he wanted to entertain. He kept moving his antenna about, finding higher and higher perches for it. Until finally he decided to stick it atop a nearby telephone pole, and fell and broke his back in the doing, and had to lie abed for months and months, the TV his sole companion. Mr. Peepers moved before him, an apparition in a Klondike storm.

For one thing, I do not desire that fate. For another, there is no point hereabouts high enough to improve our reception. Still, the family persists. The boy: "Why don't you just try it, huh? You won't know till you at least try it."

I perceive that he and his sister have taken to sneering at me behind my back and that, out of hunger for cartoons, they have come to regard me as indolent. This is not the case. It is just that television and I are the same age and I see in it the same flaws I find in myself: neither of us has gotten very far down the road. With patience, you can find in television a shining hour with the same surety you can find a diamond in a dunghill the size of Texas. I do not like its mentality, nor mine. I sit before a fire in a house situated in pastoral splendor, a thundershower playing loud my roof, and what large thought comes to mind? "That's a hell of a rain!" An actor commits suicide in Madrid and leaves a note: "I am bored and I have lived enough." That night, on the television news, the resonant voice of authority tells me: "It was an apparent suicide. He left a note that said, 'I am *boring* and I have lived enough.'" To foul a man's last words! "Good evening. Two hundred and thirteen persons were killed in a jetliner crash in Peru today. A triple murder in the southern part of the state. And the Braves win again! Ta-da! Ta-da! Ta-da!" I spoke with the weatherman who sent us running for our lives last spring with a false tornado alert. What sensitive equipment picked up the storm? "I just went out and looked at the sky." I have no interest in the birth of Bunker's grandchild, the mawkish words of John Boy, the magpie Mary Hartman. But this is my saw, not the children's, and, like the children, I miss the cartoons.

There is no solution here. Nothing short of erecting an antenna on the highest oak atop the highest ridge will clear the images on our screen. For as long as we live here, we will live without benefit of a sharp picture, as they call it in the department stores. The children will just have to understand that. At present, they do not.

Wife Wanted

Sometime within the current moon, Henry Moncrief's brain cracked with the longing for a woman. It came to him that he wasn't cut out to live alone, to drive a dozer eleven hours a day moving a half-million yards of dirt so someone could build a dam, only to go home to his twelve-by-seventy-two-foot tan and ocher trailer to find the commode stopped up, grease on the stove, a dirt dauber asleep on his parchment lamp shade.

Diversions, for a time, kept the real problem from Henry Moncrief's mind. He is not the type to sulk. He is a self-described old country boy, rough and tough, mean as a skunk, who would just as soon wrestle an alligator as not, who has never backed down from anything, though he wishes he had, once or twice. He found ways to occupy himself most of the summer, when the trouble was playing peepeye with his consciousness. If all else failed, he could kick the empty quart can of Shell 30 weight motor oil round his yard.

He spent a lot of time watering his azaleas and petunias and marigolds and lilies, and he grew tomatoes and peppers. He could sit in his folding aluminum lawn chair and stare at the single tree plow propped against the scrub pine, or fondle the old rusted out single-shot .22 rifle that usually lies in the grass near the Number Two washtub filled with Schlitz and Nehi cans. He watched the

fireflies, saw the goldenrods across the sand road disappear in the darkness, heard the old people at dusk, walking back from fishing in the Flint River.

All of a sudden, Henry could stand it no more. His self-image was of a man who "gets out and sweats in the dirt and gets home at night and there's nothing and stuff just keeps piling up, piling up, and I'm going buggy!" He walked straightway to the back of his trailer, rounded up some scrap boards, some white paint, some green paint, a brush, nails and hammer.

With zeal, with single-minded, fed-up conviction, he broad-stroked his yearning on a homemade sign: "Good wife wanted—New or Used. 886-3653." And posted it out front on Highway 128. And reached that night in his sleep the contentment that few thirty-four-year-old men will ever know.

The phone rang the next day but Henry Moncrief was not in his trailer to answer it. He must rise at five and drive 102 miles to Sandersville, where he ascends his dozer for full day's labor. He does not get home until 8:30, 8:45, when he stops to pick up a chicken dinner, packaged in a plastic plate and cover. But for the rest of that night—until 3:30 A.M., in fact—his telephone rang to him, sang to him a jangling rhapsody of love.

The old, the young, the divorced, the Christian, the heathen, all called. "Uh, hello," they began timidly, "are you the one with the sign?" "Uh, yeah, kinda," Henry replied, uncomfortable at first but soon growing used to it.

Henry Moncrief had a new notebook special for the endeavor. He took down their names, ages, height, weight, color of eyes, address, telephone number, number of children, if any. He told them in return that he was six feet tall, dark-complected, dark-eyed and not in the least bit hurried to make a decision. He did not tell them that he is gentle natured, right intelligent, strong of back and bicep. It could be assumed they imagined all that, and more. Amor de Cosmos, lover of the world! Henry was in heaven.

Henry went to work red-eyed and white-faced from lack of sleep but he did not complain to his colleagues, fellow heavy equipment operators. The nocturnal attention that would come at day's end made the hours fly. Soon he was home at the telephone again. "Uh, hello. Are you the one with the sign?" "That's me," he would reply in a clear, confident voice.

The local newspapers discovered him on his third night of telephonic mate auditions and made Henry Moncrief out to be quite a case. They took his picture, standing next to his sign. The wire services, the Associated Press and United Press International, transmitted pictures of Henry and his sign across the land and into Canada. It was this attention, this great publicity on a slow news day, that sacked Henry's tidy little plan.

Women with strange accents began calling. To a man born and reared in Roberta, Georgia, a man who went through tenth grade here and spent his life, with the exception of a hitch in the Navy, in this neck of the woods, a New Jersey voice is the voice of a Czech, so foreign it was to Henry's ears. They called from Eugene, Oregon, from Canada, from California, Pennsylvania, Oklahoma, New York, a nonstop night-long talkathon in which Henry had to describe himself, describe himself, describe himself. He tore down the sign.

But still they call. And each night when he gets off the dozer and gets his packaged dinner and gets home, he finds the mailbox full of strawberry-scented envelopes, an occasional Chanel No. 5, once in a while a Toujours Moi. The wire service photographs bore his address. This flow of affection has turned relentless.

So it was night before last as Henry sat before his television set, his fried chicken dinner untouched, Billy Graham preaching on screen, Henry hearing the unceasing telephone. "I hope you don't mind this ringing," he said. "It's gotten completely out of hand." The telephone sat quiet a second, started again.

"Tell you what," Henry said, his voice trailing off as he went to the kitchen, fished a screwdriver out of a drawer, came back and disconnected the phone. A muted ringing could still be heard, coming from a second telephone in the bedroom. He has not yet had the heart to disconnect that one. The country's lonely are reaching out to him. Sleep has become so precious, and waking so difficult, that he has strung his wind-up alarm clock from the ceiling, so that it dangles just six inches above his face, screams at him like a raucous factory whistle.

"Nobody really knows what hell and torment I've been going through," Henry says, retaking his seat, propping his feet on the coffee table. He wears construction boots with the tongues hanging out like the tongues of hard-run dogs. He sifts through the day's mail. The reason he started this business, he says, "is there's not what you might call much of your dating material here in Roberta."

A letter from Alhambra, California, a letter from Danville, Virginia, a letter from Johnson City, Tennessee. A letter from the National Life & Insurance Company. "Whups," Henry says, "I don't think this one belongs in this stack."

A crank letter: "Female. Albino. 35 years old. Lovely fine features except for: Triple chins, one brown cross eye, one blue glass eye, hook nose, buck teeth, and attractive, long hanging ear lobes."

A very literate letter, with a hint of sarcasm, from a schoolteacher in Richmond. Henry Moncrief reads it, grows thoughtful. "Why in the hell would somebody with those qualities write me without thinking it was some idiot put out that sign? I mean, this is what bothers me. Why do I get such high class people? Schoolteachers!"

A nice letter from a bank clerk in Philadelphia. She enclosed an Olan Mills color photograph of herself, wearing cat's-eye glasses and an up-do hair style, brown hair, face flat as a griddle. "Not bad," Henry says, scrutinizing.

He volunteers that he thinks he has narrowed the field to three, one of whom lives in Georgia. He will make a decision soon. He is convinced that, for all the trouble, he will find a wife this way. All the culls will get a mimeographed turndown. He has not composed it yet.

Now, with *Hawaii Five-O* going off the air, and the telephone ringing in the bedroom, Henry Moncrief decides to call a halt to the whole mess. He directs me, "Put this down." He chooses each word with care:

"Due to the number of letters—no, make that, due to several hundred letters—and some thousand telephone calls . . . nation-wide . . . including Canada . . . I think I have enough material here to fulfill my advertisement."

There, then, it is done. The contest is over. Sleep is at hand. I the chosen messenger prepare to depart into the gnat-filled night. Henry gives it one last thought. Never has the common man been so courted. "Make that," he says, "after next month, no more letters or phone calls will be accepted."

Church

A family's religious leanings are a family's personal affair, and I choose not to go into ours, except to say our arrangement is rather informal, loose. What I'm getting around to is recording that on a recent Sunday my eight-year-old boy left the fold. Made himself a better deal. We had read that many churches in the country, disturbed by empty pews, had started bussing youngsters into the congregation. The churches were offering candy and field trips to entertaining places, according to one newspaper account. Call it bussing for Jesus.

My son struck his own bargain with a gentleman who came calling. They would all go to a roller-skating rink on Friday night and on the following Sunday he would be picked up by the church bus and transported to and from services.

He went roller skating and got in about eleven. He had in the course of the evening fallen on his tail and fallen in love. However, come Sunday morning, his passion for the young lady, and the church, had cooled. The bus rolled up and he walked down to the road and told the driver he had to think about it some more. He did not board.

There followed one more bargaining session. The deal was this: In exchange for three Sundays in church, he would be taken to a vast amusement park downstate for an entire day of fun. Since the boy had shown himself shifty, it was requested that he board the bus three straight Sabbaths, and then they would make the trip to the amusement park. The boy, sliding easily into the role of negotiator, said that it should be the other way around, and held firm. And there it still stands.

Measurement

Mr. R. E. Morse, the leatherworker who recently moved to our community from Iowa City, Iowa, stopped by last night to confide a problem of enormous proportion. Mr. Morse sat with us a long time before letting go his trouble. We could see that he was bothered, because he usually holds up his end of the conversation, but last night, through much of his visit, he simply stroked his full black beard. Now and then he shifted his ponytail from his right shoulder to his left, and back again.

Finally, after feinting to leave, and rejecting coffee, he sat once more and blurted, "A man came into the shop today and asked me to make him a *sixty*-inch belt. SIXTY DAMN INCHES! And he wants a landscape on it. Forty-eight inches is about my limit."

"A man with a girth of five feet," I said. "My lord."

"What a monster!" my wife said.

Mr. Morse had given this assignment his all. The belt in its current state bore trees and horses and cows and dogs and rivers and cowboys and teepees and Indians and deer and mountains. Yet the landscape stopped twelve inches shy of its ordered length.

"A train," my wife said. "An old-time Western train, with buffalo alongside, and perhaps a gang of desperadoes on horseback, guns ablazing." Mr. Morse was delighted, and relieved, by the suggestion. He left us to pursue his craft.

It is problems like this—no, to hit the nail properly: it is the solution of a problem like this that makes me feel my wife and I are making this a better world in which to live.

Coon Hunt

It began as all coon hunts must: coon hunt talk in a kitchen, the coon hunter's friends recalling, corn-pone fashion, the best and the worst, the coon hunter's wife paying it no mind. The women seem resigned not to let this seasonal affair upset them. The men just leave after sundown and return at some ungodly hour, sometimes dragging with them the smelly kill, proud of nothing. That's all there is to it.

"Tell you 'bout the man had a monkey was a crack shot?"

"Naw, Bill, tell it."

"Tell 'em the one 'bout the monkey, Bill."

"City boy comes to the country wants to borry this monkey. So he takes the monkey and his hound in the woods and, uh, directly, the dog trees. Monkey goes up with his pistol and nothin' happens. City boy waits around and waits around, monkey up there in the tree, and after while the monkey comes down and shoots the dog with his pistol. Ol' boy takes that monkey back to the man what owns it and says: 'Your damn monkey killed my dog!' Ol' boy owns the monkey says, 'One thing I forgot to tell you. That monkey can't stand a lyin' dog.'"

I ask, "Where ya'll been all day?"

"Huntin'."

"Huntin' what?"

"Deer."

"Deer season open?"

"Is for bow and arrow."

"You use a bow and arrow?"

"Nope."

"What happens if you get caught with one you shot?"

"You can always stick a arrow in it."

Hunt time. Hunters check flashlights, load guns into pickup trucks, agree on where to rendezvous. One transfers a light ring of cornbread crumbs from around his mouth, there since supper, to his shirt sleeve. A car and a truck crank and leave in the night. A third truck will not start. "Flooded?"

"Smells like it."

"Let's give her a minute."

In a while, she starts. Driver says, "We shoulda got some gas. She's settin' dead on empty." On empty, he drives to the meeting spot, a hill above a former forest, the timber now cleared and piled in mounds the size of country grocery stores. "Ready?" Four hounds (three blue ticks and a red bone) are loosed from the back of the covered pickup. In moments they have crossed the cleared land and hit the woods, making their well-rounded, scalded dog tones.

The hunters, eight in all, a pack, really, pick their way down a rutted slope. The veterans listen hard to the hound cacophony. "What you figure, Verlin, fox?"

"Mebbe. Didn't have no trouble with 'em last year. This year, two of 'em took to runnin' fox."

One man talks directly to the dogs, the dogs a quarter mile away, the man all but summoning the diety's aid. "Don't cross the branch. Stay on this side. Whoooooooo! Don't cross that branch."

"What's across the branch?"

"Whole bank of ivy."

"Ivy?"

"Whoooooooo! It's a nice un too!"

The baying grows fainter. "Uh-oh boys, they crossed the

branch. Might's well go on." The men move off, walking as fast as men can. Light beams show clear thickets, briars, a downed oak, dead, lichen-covered. Over the oak, through the thicket, the thicket stealing a red wool cap from a hunter in the rear; over the branch and up a slope, the hounds baying loud from somewhere high above. "What you figure, Bill, sinkhole?"

"Yep. Sounds like one, maybe two of 'em, found a sinkhole. Nope. They're movin' on."

Now up, the hunters go, up a ridge with a pitch steep as a schoolyard slide. Man down. Tripped by a holly bush. "Yu'all right?" "Yep. Just knocked the wind outta me." Man whacked in the eye by a mimosa sucker, bent double by the man in front of him, then let go without regard for the rear guard. Whap! "Unh. That uz a smart un."

Everyone present and accounted for, and lying down, at the top of the ridge. Below (you could see it if the ridge were bald) is Helen, Georgia. Think of the United States as a side of beef with Maine as its head and Baja as its tail: these men, then, lie on a pimple on a brisket on a night cold enough to slaughter. To borrow a forty-year-old line from seventy-seven-year-old E. B. White: The stars hang close; some fall.

"Leaves are dry. Hard for the dogs to get the scent."

The dogs' hollerings are distinctively different. A man hollers, "TRReeeeeeeeeee!" Coon has been found in a branch bottom. At dash's end, six flashlights add a halo to the crown of a sweet gum. "Look at them eyes. Would you look at them eyes! How many you count?"

"Three."

"You mean there's a one-eyed coon up yonder?"

"Nope. Three sets of eyes."

"Three coons. My-my-mercy-me-my!"

"What you figure, Bill, bunch of kittens?"

"Mebbe."

"Reckon the sow's up there?"

"Hard to tell."

"Walk him down, Bill, walk him down." By flashlight, Bill sights down the barrel of his .22 and cracks one off. The dogs, standing on hind legs, embrace the tree with their front paws, heads thrown back, noses straight up, vocal chords employed.

Bill's slug does not stir the coons. He fires again. Again. He is trying to get one coon down, alive, so he will fight the dogs. This sort of scrap, with a live, mad coon and a pack of hounds, does not last long. But for its duration it is intense and vicious. The coon will take to its death a chunk of dog lip or ear. Bill has to hit one to bring it down. The coon falls thirty feet, flashlights illuminating the descent of a gray and black blur, and the dogs are on it. The dogs chew at it, fight over it, as they would a house shoe filled with hamburger. Men move in and separate victim from vic tors.

Another shot, another fall, another scrap, another kill. The dead coons are laid over the Y branch of a bottom sucker. Repeat.

"Now, we ain't gonna tell any so and so we got 'em all from the same tree. Are we now?"

"Nope."

"Nope."

"Nosireeeee."

All the hunters, save the hound owners, have driven away in search of another hunting ground. Three hounds are penned in the back of the truck. The fourth hound has not returned. You can hear her, way far off.

"Hee-uh!" The owner hollers. He whistles. Hollers more. Calls and calls. The dog moves farther off.

"Tell you 'bout the man had the finest coon dog in the country?"

"Nope."

"This dog would bring a coon down, break its neck, fuck it and throw it in the sack. Fine dog. Pretty dog, too. Ol' boy was out huntin' with him one night, coon got out on a branch, and they couldn't get it down. Ol' boy laid his gun down, climbed that tree and shinnied out on that branch. Branch starts to crack and the feller's gonna fall and he commences hollerin', 'Shoot the dog! Shoot that dog!' "

The recalcitrant hound returns after a forty-five-minute stroll through the woods. Owner grabs dog by the collar and jerks it toward the truck. "Get in, you bitch," he says.

Story, Made Up

The old Ford pickup came down the dirt road doing fifty miles an hour, leaving a long, high trail of dust. There were six women in the back of the truck and all clung hard to the sides as the driver recklessly negotiated the curves, here and there fishtailing the truck. The women sat on slop buckets turned upside down. Mildred held her large straw hat between her knees so it would not blow away. She was rehearsing in her mind what she would say to the driver's boss. I'm going to call Mr. Malcolm tonight, she thought. And I'm going to give him down the country. After I tell him exactly how this boy drives, I'm going to tell him none of us is going to work his fields anymore until we get a safe ride. Wait till I tell Ned about this!

The truck topped the last hill before Mildred's house and she could see Ned lying in the front porch swing, a newspaper spread across his chest. He was asleep. The driver waited until the last possible second to apply brakes, and the truck skidded sideways, its tires flinging rocks, the truck coming to stop inches from the mailbox. The sound woke Ned, and he was in the process of sitting up when he heard Mildred scream, "Reckless punk!" and the truck sped off, jostling the women against one another.

"I never!" Mildred yelled at Ned. "I swear! Never! I never!"

Ned let her reach the porch before he said, "Don't work your-self into a state, Mildred."

"Did you see that?" Her voice was a wail. "Did you see the way he drives? I swear! It makes me want to kill him!"

"Bill Handy died yesterday," Ned said. "It's in the papers."

"Oh, Ned," Mildred said, her voice calming. "I'm so sorry. You must feel awful."

"Bad news."

"You want to go to the funeral?"

"I think it'll be in New York."

"Oh," she said.

"Yeah," Ned said.

"Come on in the house. I'll make your supper."

They went into the kitchen and Ned settled into his reading chair, a big, overstuffed affair that he had reupholstered three times himself. This last time he covered it with a soft brown cor-duroy and in six months he had already worn the wale off the seat cushion. He liked reading in the kitchen while Mildred cooked. Many nights, he read aloud to her. This afternoon, hurt by the death, he had gone to the garden and picked a pail of purple-hulled peas. He had sat in his chair and shelled them while the "Memphis Blues" played in his head. The peas were in a pan on the stove, ready to be heated, and Mildred was pleased that her husband had done that for her.

"Ned," she said. "What if I gave you a good shave. Make you feel better."

"Naw," he said. "I think I'll let it ride another day. No point in it."

Shaving was one of many things that Ned despised and would not do for himself. Mildred kept a straight razor and a shaving cup on the sill above the sink. It was she who decided when Ned would be shaved and she who did the shaving. "Yes, he is a baby," she once told her women friends. "In many respects, he is just a sixty-two-year-old baby. But I decided long ago that no other man would do and I'm still sure."

Mildred began cutting up a chicken that she had left out to

thaw during the day. She had fetched it from the freezer before going to work, knowing that if she had told Ned to do it later in the day he would have forgotten. As she worked, she tried to think of something that would raise her husband's spirits. He was sitting in his chair, not reading and not talking, the "Memphis Blues" playing in him.

"Ned," she said, "I'm going to fry the whole chicken and what's left of it will be in the icebox. When you make your lunch tomorrow, I think you ought to eat the chicken because I know something that'll go really good with it. I'm going to put a bottle of Chablis in the icebox tonight and it'll be nice and cold when you're ready for lunch tomorrow. How does that sound?"

"Where'd the wine come from?"

"Remember? You got a whole case of it for your birthday from that friend of yours runs that gallery in San Francisco. Remember when they delivered it you put *five* bottles in the icebox and then you got so messy? You got sick. Anyway, you were so funny that night, before you got sick. Lord, we had a good time."

"Hell, I'd forgotten," Ned said. "It's been months. Let's put a couple of bottles in now and have some tonight."

"I have to work tomorrow."

"Just a glass or two with me, Mildred."

They had tiny portions of chicken, peas and potato salad, and Mildred went to bathe while Ned cleaned the table and washed the dishes. Ned got two dusty wineglasses from the cupboard beneath the sink and washed them. They were crystal and he noticed that one had a crack along its side. They were the last of a large set that had been in his family. He filled a milking bucket with ice and scrunched the two bottles of cheap wine down the bucket. Then he went to one of the three rocking chairs on the front porch and waited for Mildred. He kept the cracked glass for himself.

Mildred came onto the porch wearing a light cotton nightgown and furry house shoes. She had picked up her robe but decided no one would see her at night on the front porch and she would be cooler without it. She took the rocker next to Ned and they sat quietly through the first two glasses. Ned smelled the clean, soap fragrance about her, and the light spilling through the window showed her face shiny. Later in the night, she loosed the tight bun, and allowed her gray hair to fall about her shoulders. Ned brushed it.

Neighbor

Grace Samples said lunch wouldn't be much. "Leftovers," she said. She took a seat next to the window, her eyes leveled on the dining-room table, a swatter in her fist. Three flies would die by her hand, having had only a look at the sirloin, chicken, pork chops, rolls, light bread, turnips, peppers, radishes, potato salad, fried green tomatoes, sliced fresh tomatoes, and iced tea.

Mrs. Samples is a sparse woman with a puckered face. Her husband, Junior, is porcine. Junior bellied up to the table. He wore no shirt, and his chest (tanned from eighteen fishing trips in the last twenty-one days) drooped on his generous stomach, which went out and out and out, touching the table, though he sat a considerable distance away. "They put me on a diet," Junior told me. Then he wadded up a lettuce leaf and crammed it in his mouth. "Whaauugh ah cah hull uh ah . . ." The translation, after he finished chewing and swallowing, was: "Where I catch hell is I eat what I usually eat. Then I eat what they tell me to, extra."

Junior speared a handsome slice of sirloin, baptized it in Worcestershire, and popped it in his mouth. With difficulty, he said, "Get me the A.1. sauce, Grace." Grace put her fly swatter down and left the room.

"Junior," I said, "do those missing front teeth ever bother your eating habits?"

"Naw," he said. "I have a little trouble eatin' fish. I have to pull my chicken off with my fanger. Generally, I just jaw down on it. Teeth are crumblin' anyhow. I figure it'd be a waste of time and money to buy the front 'uns now. I'm gonna wait till they all go."

Grace returned with the A.1. sauce and Junior poured the goop all over his steak and it ran off the sides of his plate and onto the table.

The Sampleses live in Cumming, a town twenty miles from us. A man-made lake separates Junior's county from mine. Despite the distance, the twenty miles and the broad lake, we all live in his shadow. Junior, you see, is our region's only celebrity. Junior is a star.

Just a few years ago, Junior was one of our poorest souls. He was the sort a wife would call shiftless, or no account, or worthless. Mr. and Mrs. Samples and six little Sampleses lived in a three-room shack on the ridge behind the Cumming Water Works. They rented the shack for twenty-five dollars a month. Junior worked sometime—sawmill, carpentry, moonshining—but didn't work most of the time. Grace worked in a pants factory.

One day Junior got drunk and said he had caught the world's biggest bass. "I drank too much red whisky," he recalls. Quickly, here is what happened: A man from the Game and Fish Commission tape-recorded Junior's lie and played it on the radio; the story, a very funny fish story, was made into a record; Junior became a comedian; the Hee Haw television program signed him up; Junior, at forty-three, had regular employment for the first time in his life. He could neither read nor write.

Junior's show, Hee Haw, came on as a rushed replacement for the ill-fated Smothers Brothers. Its corn-pone style ("Do you file your nails?" "No, I just clip 'em and throw 'em away.") caught on, and the show enjoyed a healthy run on the CBS network. The network canceled *Hee Haw* after a few years, and it went the syndication route, where it appears to be doing comfortably.

A blond cherub bounded through the front door as we were finishing lunch. She is Junior's granddaughter. "Hee Haw!" she hollered, waving an envelope. "Hee Haw!" The mailman had come, bringing Junior's weekly $258.09. This is how much he is paid while the reruns are being shown. "This'll buy fish bait and flour," he said. "Easiest goddamn money I ever seen."

He is paid $650 a show for twenty-six shows a year. He makes another $10,000 to $20,000 from commercials. Back in 1967, he and Grace together made $5,000. It could be said that Junior is a three-hundred-pound king of sloths.

Junior planted a toothpick between two of his remaining, though crumbling, jaw teeth and asked me, "Y'awna see my house?" The tour began. It is a four-bedroom brick, with den and basement. There are four freezers in the basement, and all are filled to brim with meat and vegetables. Going down the stairs, I told Junior the freezers looked like coffins there in his dim basement. He said nothing. I pressed, not really knowing why, and said they were coffins, in a sense. He was keeping dead deer and dead fish, dead pig and dead cow in them. Junior said, "Y'awna see my guns?"

We inspected rifles and shotguns and pistols for quite a while. Junior said he was afraid someone would try to rob him and he wanted to be ready for the son of a bitch. I told him the son of a bitch wouldn't have a chance, because Junior had within reach the aggregate of a nation's military strength. Junior said I was right, that he would kill the son of a bitch first and ask questions later. There is a gun in every room. He has two .357 Magnums, a .22, four .38s, five .25 automatics, a .30-.30 with a 30-cartridge clip ("That un'll bring down a house," he said) and a derringer and a whole mess of others. In his bedroom, there are three pistols in and around the nightstand. In the bathroom, there is a pistol in a holster on the back of the door. You can grab it easily

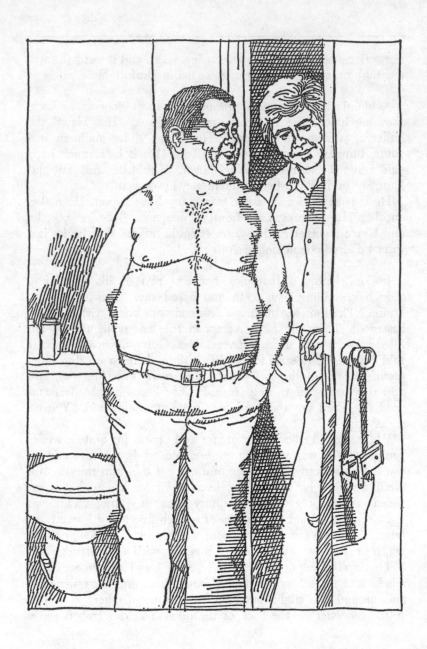

from the john when the door is closed. Junior said he had thought about it a long time, and had finally concluded that the john would be the only place the son of a bitch could have found him helpless.

We finally got off the subject of guns and went out back of the house. There is a two-story garage out there that houses Junior's $5,000 bass boat. The boat contains an AM-FM stereo radio and tape deck, two large, expensive, chocked-full tackle boxes, a .357 Magnum, pork and beans, potted meat, sardines and a jar of mustard. "Ever time I take a notion I want sompin'," Junior said, "I just go hunt around till I find it. I got anything I ever need, I reckon. I don't have to borry nothin' no more. Y'awna see my dawgs?"

We drove through the nut grass on the back half of his three-acre spread, and Junior stopped the Suburban at the pen he had built for eight newborn hounds. Junior unzipped his pants and peed on the weeds. "I got to get shed of their mamma," he said, zipping up. "Y'awna see my garden?"

The ground was moist. We walked all the rows, and Junior's stubby, alabaster-white hairless legs carried him quickly, even though his bare feet sank four inches with each step. He left tracks like craters.

"Lettuce look like they're gonna head up," he told me. "Got two rows of sweet taters over yonder. Acre of corn. Butter beans. Okra. Squash. Cucumbers. No green beans. Don't like 'em. Had a bait of 'em when I wuz a kid. Got four rows of popcorn. Watch yourself you don't mar up here . . ."

We talked until the sun went down. Junior was going fishing. I wished him good luck, and asked him one last question. I asked him whether there was anything in the world that he desired but did not have? "One thing I want and there ain't a chance in hell of gettin' it," he said. "I want a damn big yacht down on the ocean I could run around in. And I'd have to have me a crew of 'bout seven to run it. All of 'em women."

The Mother Earth News

I have chosen to include here a magazine story I've just done on the publication The Mother Earth News. *Largely because of* The Mother Earth News, *we, and countless others, live today in the rural areas our fathers had to abandon to make a living. Enough.*

There was a high crime rate in the town where Leon Blythe lived until he was thirty-seven years old, and the sidewalks, though well lit with yellowish, high-intensity, anticrime lights, bore few pedestrians in the evenings. Leon and his wife, Gail, and their four children had moved seven miles out to a Detroit suburb called Royal Oak; they and 120,000 other people. Leon's son Jeff could not make the football team at his school because the competition was so stiff. There were 3,700 students in the school. Leon was working sixty-seven hours a week as a machine-shop supervisor when he bought a twenty-eight-foot sailboat, only to find that the water near him was thick and oily. Back home in Royal Oak, he marked time in a rear corner of his forty-by-one-hundred-eighty-foot lot, eating Rolaids and drinking Maalox. His stomach pain was constant.

Leon's father had left the Carolinas in 1921, becoming yet another passenger on the migration shuttle north. Ultimately, he hooked on as an immigration officer in Detroit and stayed with the job until he was sixty-five. Then he and Leon's mother bought a lot in Florida and drove south toward retirement. Leon's father died en route from a heart attack. He was sixty-five and a half.

Leon turned to feeding his mania for a simpler life by reading publications like *The Mother Earth News*—"Mother tells you how to do for yourself, consume less, live a richer life and love it more!" An advertisement in the "Contact" section of one issue particularly appealed to him. The ad sought someone to share a thirty-six-acre farm in the mountains outside Lenoir, North Carolina. The ad closed with: "Though we're always open to social experimentation, we desire privacy and a traditional family structure. Bob and Ina."

Bob Holland, son of a $50,000-a-year executive with General Electric, had bought the farm in 1970. He had quit his job teaching in the public schools of Charlotte, North Carolina, and his wife, Ina, had quit her job pushing insurance for Liberty Mutual, and they had moved into a three-room shack on their new $7,000 spread. Largely through the help of *The Mother Earth News*, he had learned about organic gardening, chickens, hogs, goats and simple construction techniques. Too, there had been a story about a business you can operate in your home, simply by renting a computer justifier from IBM and setting type for local offset printing companies. Bob and Ina turned the suggestion into a $9,000-a-year business for themselves. Bob, thinking of his dad, was convinced they had made the right decision.

Years ago, the elder Holland was so proud of his job that he would not allow any appliance but GE in his house. He would work ten hours a day and then come home and spread his papers out on the kitchen table and give the company the extra mile. He did this until he was fifty years old.

Then, suddenly, Mr. Holland was no longer in charge of two thousand men. He no longer had a secretary to himself, but was told to share one with another executive. At his age, he was given a new assignment that involved extensive travel. Most of his old friends, fellow engineers who joined the company after World War II, had sniffed the wind and quit, or had been fired. He had

a new boss, a young man, who was leaning on him. The psychi-
atrist came first, followed by the tranquilizers. "He used to be so
proud of those jet engines," Bob recalls. "He used to look up at a
plane and swell up, just knowing he had a piece of that action."

Bob figured moving back to the land to be a sensible step toward avoiding what had happened to his father. But the typesetting business and the demands of the farm were more than he and
Ina could handle alone. So they advertised for a partner, and
Leon Blythe and his family drove south last year to the region his
father had left. Using *The Mother Earth News* as blueprint, the
Hollands and the Blythes appear to have reached the edge of near
idyllic existence.

The man who is responsible for the union just described has
come south too. Only John Shuttleworth, owner, publisher and
editor of *The Mother Earth News*, has found no such peace of
mind. He is working eighteen-hour days in his plant in Hendersonville, North Carolina. "I'm the guy with the magic words," he
says. "So I'm doing a lot of editorial work. I'm using it to the
maximum.

"Basically, more than the maximum because I'm hurting my
health. I'm almost to the end of going one hundred fifty per cent
capability. . . . I'm sacrificing my health. I get to the point where
I make myself physically sick. I have diarrhea. I ache all over, just
like giving yourself a bad cold."

John Shuttleworth, son of an Indiana full-time tool and die
maker, part-time farmer, had worked in dozens of jobs and had
managed to see a good bit of the world before he and his wife,
Jane, started *The Mother Earth News* in January 1970, in
Madison, Ohio. "The big story here is that Jane and I started to
publish a newsletter in our spare time, and you see what it turned
out to be," he says. "We started out to do something in our spare
time and we fell off the edge of the earth. The tremendous
demand. All we've done is try to fill the demand. We've become
our own Ford Foundation. The money the magazine generates we
put into our projects: the car (a prototype powered by methane

gas), the solar energy experiments . . ." His business, he says, is a time-gobbling monster.

The Shuttleworths had a total cash flow of $370 their first month of operation. Through the fantastic success of "The Whole Earth Catalog," they had seen the market open up in the alternative lifestyle publishing business. They quit their public relations jobs and borrowed money from parents, in-laws and a local loan office with an interest rate so high it might have been called the Rack and Wheel Loan Co. Exactly four years later, the cash flow for the month was $261,000. There is a graph on the wall of the Hendersonville office that charts the magazine's success, in subscriptions and income. The graph is twelve feet high. The lines take no dips.

Their operation includes the magazine, with a circulation of 200,000; a syndicated radio show, running on about one hundred stations; a syndicated newspaper column, running in about one hundred newspapers; a mail-order bookstore; a distributing company with 2,500 dealers; a printshop; and their mail-order hardware store, Mother's General Store in Hendersonville.

"I don't want anybody to ever feature us as being great world saviors and all that crap," Shuttleworth says. "We're just trying to save our butts. Trying to get things set up so that when I get to be an old man, I'll be a good old man, which I won't be at the rate I'm going."

Thousands of letters have reached Shuttleworth, all saying that thanks to him personal freedom and happiness have been found. "Great testimonials . . ." he says. "People love what we're doing. That's nice. But we're more self-serving than that. We're just trying to get the numbers on our side so that more than half the population believes in the gentler way of living and the more ecologically sound way of living. There's no great vision involved. We're just little people in way over our heads on a job a lot bigger than we are."

Shuttleworth is obviously a harassed man. He'll give you that "don't feature us as saviors" stuff, and a half hour later he will say, in a telephone call to the West Coast, "We got to present a

united front against the world." At one o'clock on a recent afternoon, Shuttleworth told me, "This is a nerve-racking business." At
two-thirty, he recalled how he had gone to sleep exhausted one recent Friday and had not awakened until Monday morning. "I feel
like I'm just about ready for the cackle factory," he said. At three
o'clock: "I can't keep up with it. I'm tired. I've aged twenty years
in the last four." He is thirty-six.

At four-thirty: "I just do it for the fun. Business is a game to
me."

"You going to work tomorrow, Bob?"

"I don't know, Leon. Maybe."

The two partners are sitting in the shade out back of Leon's
trailer, sipping Leon's homemade rosé. Leon had done some work
that morning on the house he is building. The fieldstone foundation is just about completed.

Leon had collected unemployment checks for a while after he
and his family arrived in Lenoir a year ago. A counselor at the unemployment office had found him a job managing a local machine
shop, for $15,000 a year plus stock options. He turned it down.
"The guy who was trying to hire me got mad as hell. He said,
'Buddy, when I was your age I'da moved across the country for a
job like this.' I said, 'Buddy, I just moved across the country to get
away from a job like this.'"

Bob and Leon prefer to work eight days a month for the local
electric company. They read meters for two dollars and something
an hour. It allows them a lot of spare time.

"Listen," Leon tells me, pouring another glass of wine, "an old
friend of mine came down from Detroit last fall. He came all the
way, and he didn't stay eight hours. I was on unemployment then,
and it blew his mind. This was someone I've known since I was
three years old. He works hard. He's got a shop. It cost him one
wife. It tore him up I wasn't working twelve hours a day. He got
here about one in the afternoon and he left at nine that night.
Eight hours he stayed."

Leon's wife, who has just collected a dozen eggs from the

henhouse, joins the group. Bob says, "Those Cornish eggs don't seem as brown as they used to." And Leon answers, "She's running out of juice, Bob. She's gettin' old."

The talk turns to local characters and recent happenings as Bob's wife, Ina, and their one-year-old daughter, Claire, join the gathering. "Now, Leonard," Bob says, "that guy's your real Daniel Boone. He'll be polite to you, but he'd prefer that you don't talk to him at all. Every once in a while you'll hear some shots on the back side of the mountain and you know Leonard is out there somewhere shooting. He keeps to himself and he reads those treasure magazines. That's about all anybody knows about him.

"A bunch of folks were up picking blackberries on Table Rock the other day when somebody saw a rattlesnake going in a hole. Everybody scattered and ol' Leonard just grabbed it by the tail and pulled it out. Snake must have been five feet long. Another time, Coy was fishing this big, wide trout stream a few miles from here when he slipped and hit his head on a rock. He was in the water, kind of dazed, when ol' Leonard walked up and pulled him out. Coy says Leonard sat him on a rock and watched him a couple of minutes and then he wandered on back off in the woods.

"Ina and I have taken to watching what we say around the house. You never know when Leonard might be wandering around outside."

Leon, who by this time is so laid back you couldn't find anybody more mellow, daydreams aloud about finishing the house and buying a couple of dozen Pawleys Island hammocks. "We'd string 'em all over the place, Bob, and just go from one to another."

It is lazy talk stretching on until supper. We are at Leon's picnic table, just a few yards from his trailer, and the 1951 Ford tractor that the two men bought is about one hundred feet down the ridge from us, tires hidden by knee-high weeds. The morning has been so quiet, all you could hear was breeze and one woodpecker, but the sun has dried the dew off the backs and wings of the cicadas, called locusts locally, and they're beginning to make a racket. "Local folk say the locusts come every seven years," Bob says. "All I know is they're playing hell with my orchard."

Below us, you can see about half of the thirty-six-acre farm. Hills of hardwood, mostly oak, surround the two-acre vegetable garden. Corn is five feet high on the top of a far hill, and the grapevines are coming up nicely down the hillside, just below the cornfield. Leon, a cigar-thin man with a thick thatch of gray hair and a full, symmetrically perfect sandy beard, talks of his inexperience with carpentry and the discovery he has made. "You can do anything you want to. And if it doesn't turn out, all you got to do is tear the sonuvabitch down."

And Bob Holland is laughing and joking and trying not to smoke cigarettes, having kicked the habit until Leon came to North Carolina, bringing with him a twenty-year association with Pall Malls. Bob has a big, open, honest, mustachioed face, slight shoulders and a frame that looks a little too fleshy, just a little too soft, for the rigorous farm chores and for having almost single-handedly finished a two-story cabin on the top of yet another hill. The appearance fools you. Follow him around, up one slope and down the next, sucking wind at his heels, he breathing comfortably. This neophyte farmer is in shape.

"There's a guy in town," Bob says. "He walks around pulling a chain. He can't wait till somebody asks him, 'Why are you pulling that chain?' 'Cause he always answers, 'Didja ever see anybody try to push one?' " While we're giggling, half high on wine, Bob's daughter, Claire, knocks over two glasses of rosé. Ina, a high-hipped dishwater blonde, scoops up the sopping kid and heads for home to bake bread. We give her a little lead time and move down to the Holland house for supper.

The fresh bread smell spills out the back door, turning us all ravenous, while we pitch in setting Bob's picnic table. The grass is thick and green here between the chicken pen and the house. A new litter of Dalmatian pups gnaw at our shoes and ankles when we sit down to a roast, mashed potatoes, green beans, field peas and carrots. It is dusk and the screech owls are serenading.

"I sure wish I was going to Hendersonville with you," Leon

says. "I'd like to meet Shuttleworth and see that operation. Did you see the latest issue, Bob? There's a good story in there on how to sex a chicken."

Bob: "No, I haven't read it yet. I noticed they're still on that radio shit, though." He is a little teed off that *The Mother Earth News* has been running stories on ham radios. He argues that the number of homesteaders with expensive radio outfits is minuscule; thus the stories are unnecessary.

In his house Bob has every issue of *The Mother Earth News*. "It's been good to me," he says. "The main thing we got from them was our typesetting business. And Leon and his family, of course. But there've been stories on keeping chickens, hogs and goats. Building farm buildings. All of it very useful. I think Shuttleworth is probably spreading himself a little thin these days, though, with all the things he's got going. The magazine seems to be suffering for it."

The plant in Hendersonville, a former dress factory still called the Ruth Originals building, is humming along with midafternoon efficiency. Sixty employes are typing, filing, packaging, answering calls and filling orders in their various, partitioned areas. The working atmosphere is Detroit machine shop dull.

John Shuttleworth, eyes moist and pink, coloring rat gray, the beginnings of a weedy black beard on his face, is explaining he moved *The Mother Earth News* from Ohio to Hendersonville because his wife is from North Carolina and for "other practical reasons." He is trying to set up a six-hundred-acre research center and he says North Carolina is a good area. "Two years ago in December we had fifteen hours of direct sunlight on those polluted shores of Lake Erie. Obviously, our solar energy experiments wouldn't go very fast in that kind of situation. We came down where you have less cloud cover."

The tract he is looking for will be one in which he owns all the land in sight. "Our work will be largely compromised if we own one slope and a few years later the other slopes fill up with Howard Johnsons and fast-food restaurants because we're a great tourist attraction. We want a complete mountain cove, so that when you go in there it's like going into another world. Where everything is solar heated, or electricity is made with our own little water plant, or we got wind plants set up on the ridge. So the whole idea is to put together a little world all its own.

"There'll be strong restrictions on what transportation is used. Probably have to walk around or use bicycles, maybe horse-drawn carriages, or electric cars powered with electricity made right there with windplants. . . . We've already planned for a second center in the Pacific Northwest, a third in Costa Rica and a fourth in New Zealand."

Meanwhile, John and Jane Shuttleworth, a small, skinny lady with a pleasant face and a taciturn personality, live in a Southern mansion in Hendersonville, an eight-bedroom place for which they pay $125 a month. Though they own the whole *Mother Earth* operation, they pay themselves $208 each a week. Shuttleworth says there will be a payoff for them someday.

"We've tried to be decent individuals and not be real bastards to work with," he says. "But I'm too damn trusting. I've had some people I should never have let in the door in the first place, and I've learned the hard way—about a half-dozen times now.

"People who love *Mother* and just can't wait to be a part of this thing are the least likely to work here. It's much better to just go out and hire a secretary or a typist who, in general, eventually becomes pretty enthused. . . . But these great idealists who think they can stay grassed out of their minds all day and play the guitar and somehow this groovy magazine gets put together. . . . They think this is some kind of never-never land. So we've had some real bad problems with that kind of people.

"We're through with those, now. We've become very businesslike in that area. We hire people who are only looking for a job. Period. They've never even heard of *Mother* before. That's the kind of people we're looking for."

Those bad employes might have gotten the idea they could enjoy their work with *Mother* after seeing the pictures of the staff that put out "The Whole Earth Catalog." That staff, working under Stewart Brand in Menlo Park, California, looked happy. Shuttleworth's crew, to a man, bear the grim look of the Detroit assembly line.

Just this afternoon Shuttleworth upbraided the manager of his General Store for having five employes "sitting on their butts." "I have to be a taskmaster," he told me. "I can't have one place working at one-third speed while the others carry the load."

And Shuttleworth has a few words about Stewart Brand, too:

"He's done some weird things. I hear he's blown his mind with nitrous oxide. He and that whole acid group, the Merry Pranksters and all that. Brand is hitting on about four cylinders these days out of a sixteen-cylinder engine. . . . The whole point is we get direct feedback that Brand is jealous of us at this point. . . . And also we got a lot of letters from people—I get so goddamned tired of that gee-whiz attitude at 'The Whole Earth Catalog'—I'd send for this stuff and it's no damn good. . . .

"The thing I've always really despised about any social element is this damn backbiting. Where everybody is calling the other guy dumb and saying you don't know what you're doing. We don't do that. I'm just giving you some personal observations here. That we see Brand is jealous of us—we don't care. I think he did an awfully good thing."

Shuttleworth calls his magazine a "serialized survival manual for the future." In that context, he argues against Bob Holland's beef that the ham radio stories are unnecessary. "I have to expand people's horizons a little bit in that I see some awful bad times coming. I mean super bad . . . on a global scale. . . . And I'm working right now to get people's eyes on what can be done, how you can keep some links with the kind of people you want to keep links with. I mean, let's face it, how many times can you tell people how to milk a goat?"

Shuttleworth goes on to talk with disdain of the "freak idealists" who are all talk and no action. "All that rhetoric they use, you know. I don't have time for that crap. I'm trying to pry people free in a way they want to be free. If you want to go raise chickens or you want a little home business in town or you want to set up a day care center or if you want to build your own house, great! I don't give a damn! That's the way nature works. I'm a farm boy. Nature has infinite checks and balances. . . ."

About criticism: "So I can't get too excited about that holier than thou attitude—you're getting too big, bringing in too many things. Either you're going to take over the world or you're not. You've got to get the culture changed. What I'm after is a power base for us. One of these days I'm going to surprise everybody by walking away from this thing. Giving it over to the people here and saying to hell with it. (Those last two lines came out of nowhere, in Shuttleworth's exasperated, contradictory fashion. He uttered them, then picked up the track again.) What I'm after is getting everybody moved over, right now, so that we lessen our impact on the planet. Either you're going to get the job done or not. And you've got to get big to do it. I'm sorry."

In late afternoon, driving back in a rain from Mother's General Store to the editorial offices, stuck in a traffic jam, Shuttleworth confides: "I've often said *Mother* has a lot more integrity than I do. . . . It gets to be a royal pain in the butt sometimes having to live up to what I have to. Sometimes I have this view of myself as an insane old man leading these squabbling children around."

Before the day is out, John Shuttleworth, the guy who brought Leon Blythe and Bob Holland together, will have said, "I'm not particularly money oriented. You see, my fortune's made. Just from the track record I got I can go to New York any day and pull down a $100,000-a-year job editing. I'm a good editor. I can do it well."

And then he will turn his attention to a new business proposal, a syndicated television show.

And that night he will seek store-bought relief from diarrhea.

Morning

October. Hickory and poplar all yellow. Maple, gums, red oak, scarlet oak, all red as a monkey's heinie. No flies outside; six inside, all surviving nicely, thank you, on a bountiful ration of sugar spilt by the children. Saw a pumpkin big as an Apollo command module down at the county fair last week. How to describe the splendid skies? Well, a great body and fender man I once knew couldn't paint a better sky than the one we had yesterday. Hardly seems to ring right. Temperature in the day in the mid-sixties, mid-forties in the night. Barometric pressure steady and holding, according to the radio. Bought a chain saw. And an eight-pound sledge and a wedge. Feel no longer like the fat old slug of summer. Felt like Charles Atlas loosed in the forest this past weekend. Cut and split firewood both days. Down in my back this morning.

Have been offered the position of my town's correspondent for a publication in a neighboring county. Too much responsibility, I feel. For one thing, I would have to go round gathering gossip. Much prefer to have gossip filter into the house in the relaxed manner in which it has been, sometimes years after the fact. For example: Heard recently from an unimpeachable source that the former fire chief set fire to, and watched burn to the ground, City Hall. Truth. Happened in '67.

The girl wakes. No, she is ambulatory, but she is not conscious.

A GI Joe, a Barbie, and some huge stuffed animal precede her down the stairs. "Cold," she says, reaching the bottom step, her eyes closed. I make her a pallet before the fire, cover her with a quilt. She looks wonderful there, blond hair spilling all over the pillow.

Gave the boy a haircut on the back porch Sunday afternoon. He winced and hollered, over and over, "Too much! You're cutting too much! Leave it long in the back! Leave the sides alone!" Oh, vanity, you call so early. All we wanted to do was give the boy a clear view of things. Now, he can see without brushing his coarse brown veil aside, but he is miserable. To him, the mirror reflects a cyclops. *Après* haircut is a hard time for every man, I suppose.

It is 5 A.M. Still very black out. The old whisky-voiced rooster is up. For the last few days, I've been imagining having a conversation with him, the two of us sitting on the front porch at dusk, drinking a stiff Tennessee bourbon. "Everything going all right with you, Ben?" I would say.

"No, it hasn't," he would say. "No, it certainly has not. On the one hand, the girls are driving me mad. On the other, I have a cold in my head. Perhaps you've noticed I've lost all sense of time. Years ago, when I was owned by old man Holtzclaw, now deceased, rest his soul, I had a head cold similar to this. Got up one morn and blowed my head off, a high, clear crow, falling like a waterfall at the end. The old man come out and threw down on me with a shotgun. Come to find out it was ten o'clock at night."

"Another drink, Ben?" I ask.

"No, sir. No, sir. Hardly touched this one. Would appreciate a little more ice, though."

They're milking up and down the road by now. "Farm wouldn't be a farm without a milk cow," Dillard Gilstrap told me. We don't have one. There is no way we could consume that much milk in a day. We buy ours for a dollar a gallon from Mrs. Seabolt. She also churns the butter and sells it for fifty cents a pound. Mrs. Seabolt is unpredictable, though. Once every couple of months she sells her cow and gets out of the business. She never offers an explanation, though I suspect she vacates the milking from time to time for the same reason I refuse to commence it. With a milk cow around, your place becomes your captor. You must be home twice a day, else your cow perishes. I also suspect old men keep milk cows around to give them reason for living, much the way a retiree continues to advise the office. At any rate, Mrs. Seabolt is presently on hiatus and supermarket milk floats our cereal.

My wife is up, standing before the fire in a long white flannel nightgown. I hate those things, but can see their benefit in a house this drafty. "Nice fire," she says, with the "nice" coming out an octave higher than the "fire." It takes her a while to find her voice after she wakes. "How did she get down here?"

"She said she was cold. I let her sleep there."

"She looks warm now."

My wife had brought her clothes and laid them on the arm of a big old tattered recliner that sits beside the hearth. She sheds the gown and stands warming her jeans and cotton shirt above the flame. She stands there firm and pink and goose-pimpled.

I must go for more wood before I wake the boy because he too dresses before the fire. I let myself out the back and see the clear, hard morning star and feel underfoot the crunch of first frost.

Firewood

High in the Chattahoochee National Forest at the upper edge of our state, three of us worked taking firewood. We used my new bile green $140 chain saw, a fuel mix of outboard motor oil and leaded gasoline, regular 30 weight oil for the chain, a half-ton pickup truck, and the weak backs of logging dilettantes. We worked on white oak and locust, taking frequent breaks to hawk and spit down the mountainside and tell one another how fine the day was and how fine the woods were and praise be to the inventor of the chain saw.

We had neither ax nor maul nor wedge and thus were either ill-equipped or overstaffed. Ideally, with three men, one could saw, one could split, and one could load. In this case, the lack of splitting tools left one man free. It was a good arrangement for the lazy, a poor one for those bent to efficiency. Somewhere down the line the wood would have to be split, else it would take too long to catch and burn in my fireplace. But I am not known for thinking ahead, and in this case, as in most others, I kept that reputation.

We were taking some of the best firewood in the United States and it was legal and it was free, compliments of the U. S. Forest Service. Until a couple of years ago (specifically, until the energy crunch) firewood in national forests was available only to the residents of national forests. It had been that way since 1897. The rising cost of fuel led, it seems, to at least one good idea: free wood for all. All you have to do to get it is work for it. I learned all this from the Forest Service office in town.

Periodically, the forest rangers go in and do what they call selective thinning, or forest management. Great, old hardwoods are felled to make room for new growth, for better stands. For the asking, a free use permit can be had from the Forest Service. All the Forest Service demands is the promise that the man cutting the wood will not take the wood to town and sell it. It must be solely for home use. But this is largely an honor system promise. If a man wanted to, I think, well, what the hell?

So we went to the forest, armed with a permit, a chain saw, and the knowledge that firewood goes for $70 a cord in the city. A cord is four by four by eight, or 128 cubic feet, whichever way it is stacked. Few full cord orders are filled in the city. Half cords (two-foot logs stacked four feet high in an eight-foot row) are what most people get. Or less. It is easy to see, and hard to reckon, how much wood there is in a pickup truck load of wood. Advertisements for "truck load of wood" are all about this time of year. Depends on the size of the pickup.

We got directions and followed them without a hitch, taking the dirt road to Cooper's Gap and driving up and up until our ears popped. We chased a muskrat, listened for songbirds, and observed that a nimbostratus, scudding with remarkable speed across the blue, looked exactly like a shark. The air was cool and the woods were quiet. The sumac blazed on the shoulders.

I read the instructions, flipped the choke on, depressed the trigger and pulled the starter and destroyed whatever peace there might have been in this part of the country. For the next hour and a half, we played hell with the oak and locust, felt our noses and shoes fill with sawdust, smelt the heavy scent of wood cut when the sap is high.

One of our number knew that the best firewood weighs over forty pounds per cubic foot and that the white oak and locust fit in this category. Also that locust is all but petrified, won't rot, hard as nails, hard to ignite, burns slow, makes good fence posts and coffins. (Out of sequence here, but a conversation at my hearth later on, the subject: locust: "Blow on it harder, dear, maybe it'll catch. My goodness, you've been at this a long time.")

We were done before we wanted to be. The truck was so loaded it looked like the bed would sink and the cab would rise. (A second condition of the permit is protect the resource. You cannot go in and overload and mar down and rut up a perfectly good forest road on a wet day. The Forest Service frowns on this. It was good there had been no rain.)

There being no work left to do, we tarried, yielding our sum knowledge of timber. It took a couple of minutes. One of us had read that the only reason the giant sequoia is still around is because its wood is lousy. The giant sequoia is only good for looking at. Nothing like being pertinent, standing nearly in rock-throwing distance of the Eastern Seaboard, talking about a California tourist attraction.

We kicked and pawed in the dirt awhile and then got in the truck to leave, vowing to return because there must be some justification for the purchase of a $140 chain saw. I burned the wood that would burn that night. And sitting before it while it burned, I read in a John McPhee story:

"A fireplace is an inefficient woodburning facility anyway. It's a romantic way to suck cold air into a room, heat the air, and send it up the chimney."

Walpurgis Nacht

The girl dressed as a witch, the boy as a pirate. Through the magic of cosmetics, we were able to give her warts and a down-turned mouth, him a beard and a heavy brow. Off we went, leaving on the porch a bowl of popcorn balls for our children's colleagues. I led the way with a flashlight. It was cold and dark. Our mission: trick or treat.

Two hours later we were back home. We had covered two miles of dirt road. We had waited too late. Most folk on this road are in bed by sundown. Starting out, the children had visions of candy untold. Coming home, they carried paper sacks filled with turnip greens. One kind old gentleman, caught just before he could hit the rack, gave them each a quarter. No one had touched our popcorn balls. We ate them.

They don't pay much attention to Halloween in these hills.

Deer Guns

The boy came down the stairs with a flashlight in his hand. "Dad," he said, panicky. "Dad. Wake up. Somebody's outside shooting a gun." It wasn't very light out, and it was raining and it was cold, just like it had been all week. I could hear the rain noise on the roof. "Here," the boy said, handing over the flashlight, "you'll need this." He was standing there in his long johns, beside the bed, and I groggily watched him rub his hands together, and then cup them and blow into his palms. I saw his breath.

Lying there, trying to get awake and watching the boy shiver and shift his weight from one bare foot to the other, I couldn't muster an acceptable thought. I remember thinking I should grab him and pull him under the covers with us. Or jump up and rush out in the rain and slay whatever manner of booger was taking potshots at the house. Then I heard the still unfamiliar explosion of a shotgun and somewhere along in here I came awake.

"It's all right," I said to him. I whispered. "They're deer hunters. Go back to bed. It's all right."

"No," he said. "I'm scared. They're close."

It was a half hour before I had planned to get up. I hate to get up before time to get up, hate it only a slight more than getting up on time. "C'mon," I said. "I'll make your breakfast." A full sainthood? An assistant sainthoodship, perhaps? Something, please, Lord, for all this trouble.

We sat there at the table, he forking pancakes and trying to drown each bite in maple syrup, me drinking coffee, both of us listening to the rain and the shotguns. He asked, "Why would anybody want to hunt in this weather?"

"I don't really know," I said, and I didn't. "I think the rain has something to do with keeping a man's scent down. Also, I guess— I've never been deer hunting, so I can only guess—you're not as likely to make any noise when the leaves and twigs are wet. You have to be very quiet to hunt deer."

"I'll bet they're hunting deer for Thanksgiving," the boy said. "The pilgrims had deer. Only it's called venison when you eat it. Can we have deer for Thanksgiving?"

"I don't think so," I said. I am not a hunter. My father was not a hunter, and that, probably more than anything else, is why I am not. I went on that coon hunt a month back to see what it was like, but not to hunt. When I read Robert Ruark I want to hunt. But the urge never lasts long enough for me actually to go out and try to bump off Bambi's paramour, or Thumper, or any of those creatures I was introduced to when I was growing up in the city and Disney was making the introductions.

Big, yellow, school bus Number Nine stopped at the house at ten minutes past seven. The boy said he would be only too happy to board today because Jule, the driver, a strict disciplinarian, had been transferred to another route. A new driver, a stout, likable fellow the kids called Earl the Pearl, was at the wheel. I waved from the porch as my scholar, who has expressed an ambition to grow up and be a rock-and-roll star, and a busfull of companions rolled off down the dirt road. I assumed we were both still thinking about deer and Thanksgiving. The rain had stopped, but the inconstant gunfire was still there. Every time it had been so long since the last shot that you didn't think you would hear it again, you did.

I went inside for more coffee while my wife scrambled her eggs. "It's dangerous," she said. "This is something I never thought about when we decided to move here. Don't you think you ought to put some No Hunting signs around the farm?"

"Maybe," I said. "I think I'm going to talk to some of the neighbors first. It's time I met them anyway."

I sat with my wife awhile longer. The heat from the stove had knocked some of the chill off the kitchen, but the rest of the house was still cold. Our girl was still asleep upstairs. When she wakes on mornings like this, she lies there watching her breath. She finds it very entertaining, this being able to blow clouds when you wake up.

I laid a fire in the living-room fireplace and told my wife to light it if she got too cold. Then I set out for the neighbors'.

Mozelle Grizzle was sweeping the porch of her three-room cabin when I got there. She was wearing an orange print dress beneath a black wool sweater, a sweat shirt, and a navy blue cloth coat. She is a tiny woman and she has silver hair, which she wears tied to the rear in a tight bun. Her teeth were provided by the local poverty program. She was using a new, stiff broom she had fashioned from the broom sedge in her pasture.

Mozelle said, "Glad to see you. Too bad my son-in-law's not here to meet you. He's gone in the truck most of the time. He's out huntin' this morning. If Tate was alive, he'd be in them woods too."

Tate Grizzle died two years ago. He had fathered fourteen children and his wife had given them all names beginning with a V. Viola. Viona. Virgil. Vernon. Violet. Verdie. Verlin . . . They had had a tough time just providing food for the family. Their cabin had burned in the fall a dozen years ago. The fire got more than their home. It got seven hundred half gallons of fruits and vegetables Mozelle Grizzle had canned, plus six churns of pickled corn. The family lived on the fine edge of starvation that winter. Tate Grizzle shot five big bucks that season. Mozelle told me this.

I asked her, "What kind of Thanksgiving did your family have?"

"We never paid much attention to it," she said. "Just kept on workin'. Lemme see. Well, all the fodder's pulled by Thanksgiving, but you've still got a lot of wood to chop. It's not a time to be on easy. Once in a while I'd make a pumpkin pie."

We sat there awhile on the front porch of her tar-papered little shack. Muslin sacks filled with dried beans hung on nails above us. Her front yard is all mud. A dozen or more white leghorns pecked in the mud, looking for a worm or a piece of grain and finding nothing.

"Well, what kind of Thanksgiving will you have this year?" I asked.

"We might have some venison if my son-in-law's lucky." She laughed, then excused herself. She had to go inside to make some catnip tea for her granddaughter's cold. Then, she said, she had to figure some way to get the baby to Lonnie Martin's house. Lonnie can cure "thrashes," a white irritation in the child's mouth. He conjures it away. She stood and I noticed the thick white sweat socks she wore, and the cheap floral house shoes, and when she went inside I got a look at the living room. There was a large gas heater in the middle of the room, and on the walls I saw three color pictures of Jesus. One of the pictures looked like it had been done in 3-D.

Next stop, Pearl Berry's house. The thick, green boxwood shrubs outside her cabin were trimmed flat as table tops. She used the shrubs for drying vegetables. Lately, she had left okra pods out to dry, intending to use the seeds next spring. Pearl Berry is eighty. She has lived in her cabin for fifty-three years. The cabin had been a store when she was a girl and she had bought candy there, tying her mule to the oak saplings out front. The oaks are tall, old and cankered now. She told me all this as we sat before her fire. Two good-sized pieces of hickory burned.

Directly, I asked her about Thanksgiving. "What did you do for Thanksgiving?"

"Worked," she said, and she got up from her rocker and poked the fire a time or two. A fresh, slim blue blaze shot up from between the back log and its smaller front companion. "Well, now," she said, "every once in a while I'd make some tarts or fried pies.

Reminds me, let me get you something." She pulled a gray wool sweater over her shirtwaist and apron and she left the room. Pearl is a short, stout woman with a round face, lineless except for the corners of her eyes, and, like Mozelle Grizzle, silver hair tied in a bun. She wore Ace surgical stockings on her legs. She came back with a half-gallon jar of dried apples. She went to the kitchen for a paper sack and returned to pour me a sackful to take home.

My wife would cook the dried apples with sugar and cinnamon. She would pour them on thin, round slices of dough. Then she would fold the dough over and make pies the shape of half-moons. The pies would go into a frying pan of hot grease for a couple of minutes. We'll do that for Thanksgiving, I thought, walking from Pearl Berry's cabin with the sack in my coat pocket. "It'd be good if you had some deer," she had told me. "You oughta be out huntin' this mornin', stead of bein' social. Such foolishness!"

Edward Carroll was sawing on a dead hickory tree behind the Wahoo Baptist Church when I got there. "It's awful to saw but well worth it," he said. Everyone in the county calls him Mr. Carroll. He is eighty-nine. "Green hickory scares me," Mr. Carroll said. "It'll pop and set your house on fire. There's nothin' finer than dead hickory."

Mr. Carroll, in his overalls and his railroader's denim coat, continued sawing. He is a frail-looking man of medium height, with a large nose that has prominent blue veins showing around the nostrils. He told me that his wife died nineteen years ago today. They lacked thirty-nine days being married forty-seven years. They had had sickness in their family for twenty-six years. Their baby had died and they had spent all their time tending to his mother and father and his wife's grandmother, all of whom lived with them. "It left me with a clear conscience," he said. "That's about all."

Mr. Carroll said he was a little nervous about Thanksgiving, because he was planning a long trip. He was going to spend the day with his niece and her family, seventy miles away. He would come back that night, he said, "because a man needs to get back to his

own limb." I asked, "Did you do anything special on Thanksgivings when your family was with you?"

"No."

"Then what made it Thanksgiving?"

"Well, the mail didn't run."

We walked across the road to Mr. Carroll's cabin, which is
heated by a fireplace and a wood stove. The old man got his newspaper out of the box and read the top headline aloud. " 'Suspect
Nabbed in Armed Robbery.' Hmmmmm. Weren't you nor me,
was it?" I shook my head. "Then we got nothin' to worry about,"
Mr. Carroll said. "Come back and see me."

The last stop before home was at Wine Sainc's house. The day
was clear and cold now. Winc Saine is sixty-two years old and
suffering from a broken foot. He sat before his gas heater in the
living room, his foot in a cast. "I took the little ol' dog out to see
if he could scare up a squirrel," Wine said. "When I stepped off
the back porch, my foot turned on me. I went flat on my belly on
that concrete. Doctor said I broke three bones." Wine Saine, a
large man in overalls, a man too large to be foundered like that,
said he would have to be off his feet for weeks.

"Got me one deer, though," he said. "Went out to that white
oak where he'd been eatin' acorns and I just sat down. Directly,
he come along and I killed him. He's an eight pointer. He's in the
freezer. Why don't you get yourself some?"

I walked home with venison steaks in one pocket, dried apples
in the other. It was good to have met these people, I thought.
Deer certainly are important up here. I did not think again about
posting the No Hunting signs until the next morning. I have yet
to post them.

Thanksgiving

"You wanta stick him?"

I said no, I didn't want to stick him.

"You wanta stick him?"

Mac said no, he didn't have his knife with him.

Our questioner pulled a Buck Ranger 112 from the sheath on his belt, bent at the knees, and felt with his unoccupied hand for the Yorkshire's jugular. Finding the vein, he severed it. Blood from the white pig, already dead with a .22 in its brain, flowed thick on the concrete floor of the swine barn, and an assistant to the pig sticker used a water hose to direct the flow toward a metal drain near the wall. "Reckon she'll weigh one seventy, one eighty maybe," the first man said, wiping his knife blade on his jeans.

When the hog was blooded, I pulled it by the hind feet to the white scales in the corner, leaving as I dragged a narrow serpentine blood stripe. She weighed one seventy-three. By some mysterious, to me, tabulation that rests on the latest hog futures figure in the stock pages of the newspaper, she cost $58.37. I wrote a check, then got in the back of Mac's truck to spread a sheet across the bed. With Mac at the front and me at the hind, we lifted the dead pig into the truck, and wrapped it with the sheet.

On the drive to the town of Cleveland, where John the Butcher lives and works, Mac told me the story of a bibulous evening when he was a young Marine. It seems he and his colleagues, and a civilian farmer who was employed by the base in a mechanical capacity, got very drunk at the enlisted men's club and came up with the notion to barbecue a cow. The civilian farmer, by now loose as a monkey, volunteered to sacrifice a member of his herd. "I mean this was cattle with a family tree like a championship dog," Mac said to me. "Ancestor after ancestor. This ass [Mac calls everyone an ass] had a stack of papers on them cows."

Mac and the farmer went off in the farmer's truck. They let themselves through a gate to a pasture and chose by flashlight a yearling with a rump defined like an apple. Apple-assed. Mac shot the cow between the eyes with a .30-.30, and he and the farmer, stopping here and there to pull on a pint of Evan Williams bourbon, managed, with great drunken effort, to get her loaded, transported, and deposited at the enlisted men's club on the military base. Others, with a high sense of mission, had dug a pit, cut the wood, and strung one-hundred-watt light bulbs round the feast area.

Shortly after dawn, Mac woke with a headache in a booth in the club. A table full covered with beer cans and whisky bottles was the first thing he saw. He made his way awkwardly through the swinging door to the kitchen and found on the floor the farmer whose cow was transformed in the night by steadier hands into barbecue. The farmer, awakened by Mac, righted himself and rubbed the matter from his eyes. His eyes were the eyes of a man sprayed directly with bug repellent. He walked with Mac out the back to the pit and sat next to it like a widow at a coffin and wept. He did not eat that day.

This story, which turned out to be slightly prophetic, which is why I mention it, was just ended as Mac drove past the chicken yard of John the Butcher and turned the truck around to back it up to the big double doors of the blue aluminum outbuilding slaughterhouse. "My man," Mac told the black butcher with the knife in his hand, Mac jabbing a thumb in my direction, "says you can keep the head and the feet. We're gonna barbecue the rest of it."

My swine now hung head down in the company of others of her generation. An elaborate system of pulleys and chains was tracked across the ceiling of the slaughterhouse. By this means, the meat was moved from scalding bath to scraper, from scraper to gutter, and so forth. Three black men, all with bandannas tied around their heads, whistled and sang while they worked. Three white men, customers, like me, stood around a kerosene heater and told deer-hunting stories: ". . . and the buck looked so good, he propped his head against a tree, and stuck his shotgun in that deer's rack. He stepped back to take a picture of it and the buck jumped up and ran off. That buck shot and killed two hunters that day . . ."

One of the butchers gave a knob on the wall a half turn and blue flames shot up from the propane gas jets beneath the galvanized tub. My Yorkshire hit the water and floated, snout up, as a fat pink crocodile. The butcher immersed her, then let her bob up, then with his knife removed a long swath of coarse hair from along her back. In seconds, he had scraped all the hair that could be scraped while the pig still stayed in the water. He pulled on a chain and got her up, dripping, steaming, and shoved her off to one side. A second man stood waiting at his station nearest the tub, cavalierly raking his fine knife back and forth over a long-handled whetstone. His job could be likened to that of a finish carpenter. He made no unnecessary stroke. He did not once cut the pig. Delicately, he removed the hair from behind the ears, in the ears, from around the nose and eyes, from between the toes. The pig, hairless, pink and still steaming, was shoved across the room to the third man. The third man's work wound up in a bucket on the concrete floor. "Say you don't want the head?"

I said no.

"You don't want the feet?"

I said no.

Mac and I drove back to my house, my pig in the rear of the truck, flat as a dog run down twelve times. The pig now weighed seventy-two pounds. "Doesn't look like any pig *I've* ever seen," the boy said on first sighting. I laid a four-by-four piece of plywood across two sawhorses, then laid the pig on the plywood. We covered it with another sheet. Periodically, two ghoul hounds from up the road came around to sniff the fare. I hit them both with rocks and had the boy stand guard, his pockets stuffed with stones. "What did the pig look like when they cut his head off?"

"Beatific."

"Be a what?"

"Happy."

Big, flat-bottomed November clouds scudded high above as I worked making firewood of two tall hickories. It was cold in the shadows in the woods back of the house. My wife had gone off to borrow a tent from the funeral home, case of rain. Mac was off rounding up tables.

In an hour, I had all the wood we would need, plus a brush pile tall as me for kindling. Even with the wheelbarrow, it took my girl and me another hour to move all the wood to the hillside overlooking the barn, a bucolic cook site mutually selected. Not wishing to tax herself, she hand-carried one small stick at a time, making no less than two dozen round trips. Mac, meanwhile, had returned with the tables and the makings for the sauce and was in the kitchen, creating. First, to give himself work space, he removed from the counter the gallon fruit jar that is home to the boy's copperhead. The snake, for all of us but the boy, is an unwelcome guest in our home. The snake, name of Beans, went quietly with Mac to a dark corner of the house where it was hoped he would live unnoticed through the next few days.

With the wood stacked, I went to the barn for the shovel and returned to dig. The girl had gone to assist Mac and I was left in the company of the aged gelding, Mouse, who stood close as possible to the barbed wire fence and focused his black eyes on my moves, his ears raising and lowering to the rhythm of my grunts. I dug the pit eighteen inches deep, four feet wide and six feet long. The horse approved. The cold red sun stayed for seconds above the woods to the west, then melted. I lined the pit on three sides with concrete blocks. I stuck five steel tubular rods crosswise over

the pit, threading the rods through the holes in the concrete blocks, then laid over the rods an iron grate we had scavenged a month earlier from the public dump. Mac came up the hill with a drop light, the type automobile mechanics use, on a long extension cord and fixed it to a branch in a mimosa tree. It was dark when we started the fire.

The kindling fired and turned to ash before the first billet was laid. More kindling. More kindling. Now a chunk of hickory. It seemed a long time before we had enough coals to shovel into the pit. The meat had to be cooked on coals, no open flame, so we would have to keep the secondary fire going the night.

The pig slid easily off the tilted plywood and landed skin side up, just as it was supposed to, on the grate above the glowing pit. We added a jury-rigged tin roof across the top, effectively holding in the heat, and returned to tend the feeder fire. My wife and children stayed with Mac and me until the moon rose, and the night grew too cold. I followed them in to say good night, and to put on thermal underwear, and when I returned to the fire Mac explained to me why it is the country is in such rotten shape and painted for me the definitive picture of the economy as seen from our hill. In short, we are now being, and we can expect to continue to be, cored.

Near midnight, two friends arrived to help with the watch. The four of us sat around our charge, talking in unnaturally low voices brought on by the late hour, looking from across the road, I assume, like cannibals hunched round a cooking missionary. The stories we told one another were randy. At 3 A.M., we turned the pig. At 3:15 A.M., we sought warmth in a bottle of antifreeze from Kentucky. At dawn, we were drunk.

From here on out, it's a blur, a time warp, gauze on the lens. I know it to be true that thirty or forty people were with us in midmorning. Below us, packs of children took turns riding the horse and swinging in the tire swing that hangs from the black walnut tree. Cars of all makes were parked neatly on both shoulders of the dirt road. The sun was brilliant, the sky blue, and no one thought, or mentioned to me at least, the funeral home tent. The pig was done and fragrant. In the last hours, we had mopped it with sauce.

In my ear, an oozing voice, Southern syrup: "Ah cain't ah-magine leavin' mah sick Daddy on his deathbed on Thanksgivin' to come up he-ah to yo' hills. But now that ah'm heah, and see all this fine fellowship, ah cain't ah-magine bein' anywheah else!"

Flat removed, dead out of it, passed out beneath the mimosa tree, guests stepping over me as they would a sack of shit.

At one in the afternoon, a shower, a headache, and obligations: someone had to carve the pig. Mac's three tables were piled pile upon pile with side dishes, everybody's best shot—the best baked beans in the Western Hemisphere, the best hot German potato salad, the best mild potato salad, the best sweet potato pie, home-made bread, green bean casserole, slaw, honey, pickles, radishes, artichokes, apples, onions, cobblers, the second-best baked beans in the Western Hemisphere . . . beer, brandy, cognac, scotch, Bourbon, rye, red wine, white wine, Pernod, Dom Perignon, pipes, cigars, cigarettes, amyl nitrate, marijuana, windowpane, sheep tranquilizers, an inexhaustible store of the tastes, good and bad, of the whole world.

Everyone got fed. Having freed my head from the mangle of the morning, I saw clearly a man, his wife and child walk to the road. Upon reaching their car, he laid his seven-X beaver Stetson on the automobile roof, entered on the driver's side, and drove away, going out of sight over the ridge, leaving behind on the shoulder of the road his mortified wife, child in arms. The only thing he left them was his hat, blown into the corn patch.

The hearty stayed late to sing songs with my guitar accompaniment and to eat seconds.

On the morning following Thanksgiving, going around the house picking up discarded jackets, abandoned children's tennis shoes, purses, scarves, garbage, and with a trip to the dump imminent, I learned from my wife that I had not eaten the livelong day of our party. Happily, she said, an entire shoulder was salted away in the freezer. Thanks, I said, but no thanks. I could find no stomach for ham.

True Story of a Neighbor Unnamed

Harley was watching *The Guiding Light* on his color television when the two debt collectors knocked at his trailer door. Given entrance, they asked where he kept his TV. "You blind?" Harley said.

With silent efficiency, one of the men unplugged the set and held the cord while his partner gathered it in his arms. "Would you get the door for us, Harley?" the man holding the TV asked. Harley opened the door and held it while they passed, one gingerly carrying the cord behind the other like someone carrying the train behind a bride.

They returned in a moment and asked for the rod and reel. "On the wall above where the TV was," Harley said. One of the men took down the fishing equipment, praised the Mitchell-Garcia reel, and said Harley must have had a fine time in the eight months since he bought the gear from Western Auto, failing all the while to make a payment.

"Yessir," Harley said. "I've purely enjoyed it." The debt collectors left and Harley made himself a mayonnaise sandwich. He ate it while sitting on the sofa, staring at the wall.

Sitcom Life

The sun was just hanging out there, a huge orange gob, about a thumbnail or two above the ridge. We judged it to be about seven o'clock, a fine Sunday morning in early winter when you honestly don't want to stay in bed. I doubt that I have ever felt better. I began whistling the piccolo obbligato from "Stars and Stripes Forever" on my way to the john. I threw open the window before brushing my teeth and noticed a screech owl, silent, asleep, on a high limb of the old apple tree that stands back of the house. We had heard his call through the early part of the night. I closed the window, so not to disturb him, and began the obligatory bathroom maneuvers.

And there in my peace came a terrible moan, followed by the sound of spasmodic thumping. It came from behind the toilet. (That last sentence strikes me as a good title for a horror movie.) I bent down, mouth full of Colgate, to find one of the kittens, apparently in the grips of some terrible illness. Ghost, I think his name was. Before that, it had been Bandit, and before that, John. My children are indecisive about names. He kicked thrice more before I could spit out the toothpaste, and then he kicked no more.

I went and got a shoe box, a shovel, and the family. We buried him beneath the tulip poplar near the barn. There were no tears.

It looked to be a clear-cut case of distemper, and the kids seemed to understand that, as my mother used to say, these things just happen.

We finished the ceremony and went in for breakfast, all of us determined to get on with this fine day. My boy said he was going into the woods and build a clubhouse. My girl said she would watch him build it, then help him play in it. My wife said she was going over to the high meadow to sit in the sun and to think about not thinking about anything. And I was going to town for the Sunday paper.

I backed the van out and headed down the dirt road, returning to the piccolo piece from "Stars and Stripes Forever," which is one of the most fun things a whistler can do. The van rolled along at a modest speed, its tires stirring dust all back of us. I saw a possum, two blackbirds, a buzzard and a dead squirrel. Approaching a slight incline, my vehicle completely lost power. I tried four times, but could not negotiate the hill. I got out to inspect the engine, which is in the rear. Instead of walking directly to the back, I headed round the front of the van, and down along the passenger's side. Maybe I thought the delay in getting to the trouble would afford time to figure a solution. At any rate, I was promptly on the ground, stunned. Some generator somewhere was shooting entirely too much juice into this electric cattle wire.

I lay there for a full five minutes and, deciding no one was going to come along to offer sympathy, I got up to stare at the engine. Everything seemed to be connected properly and I knew nothing else to check. So I walked home and crawled into our faithful, dependable, fifteen-year-old sedan. It sports a coat of pigeon droppings. I made an obscene gesture at the abandoned van as the old chariot carried me comfortably past.

The front page of the Sunday paper played Cassandra for the world. Times are hard all over, each story said, and there is no relief in sight. Still, the Sunday paper is addiction. I would read even the darkest accounts and shake them off by thinking, "Long as I'm feeling okay . . ." A selfish outlook, but useful in this parlous age.

About two miles from home, as I was listening to a sermon on the car radio, the left front shock absorber collapsed in perfect harmony with the water pump on the engine. I walked the rest of the way, carrying under my arm the newspaper lousy with depression. I was sleeping soundly at noon when the heavy rains came and washed away the gravel I had used to fill the ruts in the driveway.

A Pony for the Boy

First one we looked at was out back of a sawmill, a little old albino Shetland with splayed legs and a gait like that of a dying ewe. Even at fifteen dollars, it would have been a sorry present for a boy expecting a stallion; son of Fury or nothing. We passed on the faded Shetland and stepped up the search.

There were a lot of pony inspections in those days. We would get in the car and drive thirty miles, expectant, happy, always to find what looked like a big, mangy, barely breathing dog. "My kids sure had a good time with him," owner after owner would say. "Course, kids're all growed up now."

Our best bet, we finally learned, would be the livestock auction in Gainesville, twenty miles from our town. My wife went and found it an affair that warrants sharp creases in your overalls and, for the men, good, close shaves. She met an old man there whose face, she said, could have outlived a dozen bodies. He told her, "Pistol got a pony for sale." The man's full name is Pistol Gaydon. He is tall, rough, grizzled, and a marksman at tobacco spitting. My wife made the trip to Pistol's farm and she called to say she had the perfect find, a sturdy Welsh gelding for twenty-five dollars. "He is beautiful," she said.

She fetched him home with the help of a friend and tied him to the porch of a neighbor's house a mile down the road. It was still seven days before time to give the boy his pony. Each morning for four days my wife went down and fed him hay, sweet feed, and water. She rode him till she was sore, fearing he might be too spirited for the boy.

On the fifth day, she found that he had chewed the rope in two and was loose. She had to search for a half hour before finding him. He was trying to nose into a chicken house. She called me and said she would be coming back down the road with the pony, and I quickly got the boy interested in shooting his slingshot deep in the woods. Meanwhile, she bridled the pony and led him past the house and up to Mac's place. I have mentioned Mac before. He is the large man who lives over the ridge back of us.

She left him inside Mac's fence for the night. We would have to continue the subterfuge only one more day, then we could unveil the surprise. The telephone rang shortly after daylight the next morning. "Hey," Mac said, "has your horse been eating green grass?"

"No," I said. "Not that I know of."

"Has he had anything he's not used to?"

"He might have gotten into some chicken feed yesterday," I said.

"You better come quick," Mac said.

My neighbor had gotten up at six and looked out the window to check on the pony. The pony had been down, rolling on his back, and he had worked himself halfway beneath the bed of Mac's truck. There was a hard frost on the ground but Mac rushed out in his undershorts and got the pony to its feet. He was leading the pony round and round his house when I got there. Mac was blue-lipped and barefooted.

We figured the pony had the colic. He was in awful pain. He would sink to his knees, crash on his side, and thrash about, hoofs flaying every whichway. In this situation, you must keep walking him until his system has gotten rid of whatever upset him. We knew that much. But our combined strength could keep him up for only short stretches. I called the veterinarian.

The vet said that we could not allow the pony to thrash about.

He would come straightaway, he said, but it was twenty-five miles and, while we waited, we had to keep the pony walking. If we continued to let him flounder, he would twist an intestine, and that, not the colic, would kill him.

So we pulled and pushed and heaved and the pony and Mac and I fell down a lot. It was nearly an hour before the vet arrived and he got out of his truck yelling, "Get him up! Get him up! I told you you have to keep him on his feet!" The vet did not hear when I explained that we hadn't the strength.

The vet, a Dr. Enley, gave the horse a shot of morphine. Then he pulled out a device called a Hot Shot, which looks like a flashlight with two prongs on the end. Its two batteries send a charge through the prongs, and, when he touched the pony with the Hot Shot, the pony bolted to its feet. The vet pumped a gallon of mineral oil down the pony's nose, to flush his system. Then he gave him two more shots. He told me to walk the pony for at least four more hours. If he can stand alone, the vet said, you can stop walking him. He said to call him if I had any questions and he left me with a vial of morphine, a syringe, and the Hot Shot.

I dragged the pony round the house until two o'clock in the afternoon, giving him morphine shots in the hind quarters at prescribed intervals. My wife would come up hourly and try to spell me, but she was not strong enough. A few minutes after two, the pony collapsed, and I could not get him up, not even with the battery shocks. He fell in a great heap, nose to the ground, his long, luxuriant winter coat, the color of pure honey, sopping wet. I sat at his nose for an hour, thinking he would get up, but he did not. The boy never saw him.

Mac called later that night. He had found another pony and he was bringing him home, with saddle and bridle. When I went up to see him in the dark, Mac's mother-in-law, an old lady everyone calls Granny, took me aside to whisper to me.

"Don't offer to pay Mac back for the pony," she said. "We all felt terrible about the other one dying. All of us chipped in and bought it."

We gave it to the boy the next day. It is brown and white, with markings similar to those of a poulan china pig. It is smaller than the first one. The boy swung into the saddle and the pony immediately reared twice, delighting the rider. The boy said it was the best Christmas he could recall.

The Cigarette Lighter

Two days after Christmas, Mac was being pressed to install the automobile cigarette lighter he had given Granny, his mother-in-law. He rang me for assistance. When I got there, I found Mac and his boy Eddie, who was home on leave from the Army, both belly down on the front seat of Granny's little car, Mac and Eddie head to head, the two of them fiddling with wires beneath the dashboard.

"I tell you what," Mac said, seeing me, sliding out, his sweat shirt crawling up his great stomach, "you go in the house and tell Granny everything's going along fine. Tell her all we need is three glasses full of ice."

Granny greeted me at the door and asked about the pony. Told the pony was doing fine, she asked about Mac's progress with the cigarette lighter. Told he needed three glasses of ice to finish the job, she said, "Well, I never." Then she said, "What for?" and I said I didn't know.

When I got back outside with the glasses, I found Mac and Eddie sitting on the tailgate of Mac's truck, a jug between them. I handed Mac the glasses and he poured three tall drinks. We drank the drinks and noticed that on a clear winter day like this, with all the leaves gone, you can see Yonah Mountain from Mac's house, which straddles a ridge. Yonah Mountain is thirty miles away.

Mac said we ought to go inside and see if there might be a football game on the television. Inside, Granny said to Mac, "Did you get the lighter in?"

"Everything's done but one little ol' thing. All you gotta do, Granny, is drop by the Ford place tomorrow and tell the man there to hook it up. He'll see what you mean. Won't take long."

There was no football game, and I excused myself, saying I had chores to do, which I did. Outside, walking past Granny's car, I looked in and saw the radio lying on the front seat, next to the unattached cigarette lighter. In the middle of the dashboard was a hole the size of a piepan, and wires were sticking out from the hole, every whichway.

The Mayor

Lately, I've been listening to the radio in the mornings. The station is in the next town. I like the program *Swap Shop*, wherein my neighbors call trying to peddle everything from plows to hot rods. (Yesterday, a woman caller got rattled when put on the air: "Uh, I got this thing in my front yard. Uh, it's my son-in-law's. Uh, it's . . . Uh, it's . . . Awwww, I can't think of *what* it is. I'll have to call you back!") And I like *Opinion*, wherein my countrymen call to complain. Here's one from early this week:

"I was coming up I-85 and this woman come up behind me. And she kept a blowin' and a blowin'. I couldn't get over in the right lane 'cause there were two cars blockin' me. She must have decided she was goin' to run me off the road. Finally I had to get off on the shoulder.

"I tell you she was goin' to run me in a ditch and kill me. So what I wanted to tell you was next time I'll have a pistol under my seat and I'll put a stop to that!"

The county agent, Whitey Butler, is a frequent guest on the *Opinion* show. Though I've never met him, I judge Butler to be a man with a fine sense of humor. The last time I heard him on the radio, a woman called to ask him how to get rid of the squirrels that were eating her pecans.

"Aw," Butler said, "just shoot the devils!"

Another woman wanted to know how to keep the birds from eating her cherries.

Butler said he knew someone who tied a cat to a cherry tree limb. That was effective until the cat tried to get down. The cat hanged himself. "It still worked," Butler said. "The dead cat up there just swayin' in the wind."

The man who holds the whole morning together, as far as we faithful listeners are concerned, is the disc jockey, Jim Hartley, who also happens to be the mayor of his town. I have met him. As fine a mayor as we're likely to find.

Hartley and I had a long talk one day about this interesting combination, this being mayor in the afternoons, deejay in the mornings. "It certainly makes you accessible," he said. Sometimes, people call while he's on the air and want their road repaired right then and there. Other times, they dredge up what Hartley calls a county affair. They need to get in touch with the county commission, not him. "I should have known I wasn't gonna get no help no way," a woman said to him recently, hanging up.

From time to time, an organization will come by with a proclamation for him to sign, bringing along the photographer from the local newspaper, and Hartley will step out of the studio long enough to sign, pose for pictures, and get right back to his job. Other times, the city will have an urgent piece of mail to get out, and a marshal will come by and Hartley will sign it, never breaking his dialogue with the citizenry.

He told me that he had been with the radio station thirty-three years, and that he only got interested in politics four years ago when he and his neighbors fought City Hall to get their road paved. The city paid them no mind until Hartley pointed out it was costing ten thousand dollars a year to maintain the dirt road. The city declared it a necessity that the road be paved, and paved it.

Between seven-thirty and nine each morning, the mayor's routine is pretty much rote. Time and temperature, records ("That was a group called Percolator with a song called 'Hot Butter.' Or was it the other way around?") and calling a local marina for the fishing report. "I weighed in one crappie at one and a half pounds. That's the only one I weighed. The rest of 'em are hearsay."

Also, the celebrity birthday of the day (entertainer Henry Morgan) and the thought for the day: "One thing about tight shoes, they make you forget your other troubles." And an occasional joke: "Did you hear about the fellow who got sick from drinking booze out of a tomato can? That just goes to show you booze won't hurt you but a tomato can. That's terrible, isn't it?" We shut-ins appreciate anything we can get.

But at nine, it's time for *Opinion,* my favorite. Hartley moderates and the audience phones in and sounds off. There is a family of regulars that calls in so frequently that Hartley has had to restrict them to three days between calls. One, code name Lover Boy, is looking for a rich wife.

And there are the back-yard squabbles. Someone will call and complain about a neighbor's dog. A few minutes later, a second caller will say, "I heard that woman complaining about the dog. And I know who she is. I recognized her voice. Well, you can tell her for me she can just go piss on herself!" Occasionally, the mayor won't be quick enough in cutting off a caller.

Hartley told me the most ridiculous call he ever received was when Neil Armstrong and company were en route to the moon. He was reporting Apollo progress when a woman called to say:

"Shame they couldn't have waited three or four days."

The mayor: "Why's that."

"'Cause we'd have a full moon by then. Bigger target for 'em to shoot at."

I feel better knowing I can tune in the mayor each morning. And I see him about once a week when I make my regular trip to the newsstand for magazines. The last time we talked, he said that there was one thing in his life he wished he could change. He said he wished the community would stop worrying about his health. He had a heart attack a few years ago, and everybody knows about it. Now, if he is late signing on the air, everyone calls his house to find out what's the matter. If he coughs on the air, or sounds a little hoarse, they stop him in the supermarket to check his health, or call his wife to make sure he has been taking care of himself.

A Day with the Vet

Jacqueline Smith, our veterinarian, got a call last Saturday from an elderly man whose Chihuahua had been chewed up by a German shepherd. When she went to work on the Chihuahua, which was about to expire, owing to a large cavity in its chest, she found the old man was preparing to shoot the shepherd. The shepherd belonged to his nephew. In return, the nephew was going to shoot the old man's cattle. A minister was called.

The Chihuahua died and Mrs. Smith left the feud in favor of a sick horse, twenty miles to the north. The horse had had a bad case of worms and he was down in his stall. He had no feeling in his hindquarters. A blood clot had caused this situation. It was messy for a while, with the horse's owner, a woman, crying, and Dr. Smith hugging her.

It came down to either investing as much as two hundred dollars for surgery on the old quarter horse, or destroying it. Ultimately, it was decided to destroy it. Dr. Smith, retiring early that night, hoped for no more telephone calls. "It hasn't been my day," she said. The telephone rang, and a woman said, "Would you listen to my parakeet breathe on the phone? He doesn't sound right." Dr. Smith listened but couldn't hear a thing.

Dr. Smith and her husband and their son and daughter came

from Michigan to our county a couple of years ago, right after she had finished veterinary school at Michigan State University. They came because some college friends had said it was nice down here, and they had left twelve inches of snow, and gotten here when it was seventy-two degrees and the dogwoods were blooming. Now her husband, Steve, is finishing his master's and will go with the county school system, and she is trying to get a clinic opened. In the meanwhile, her practice is in her car, a Ford, and on her dining-room table. Her anesthesia machine is next to the table, and her X-ray machine is in the garage. There is a garbage can full of sweet feed, which she uses to summon recalcitrant horses, next to the garage door.

I went on a few calls with her one cold wet day earlier this week, and I would like to assume, for a few small paragraphs, the role of veterinary biographer:

We headed out in the rain, Dr. Smith stopping to get a bucket of sweet feed. Her sister, Jan, down from Michigan, and Jan's friend, Beth, were along to help out. One of the nice things about being a woman vet, Dr. Smith said, driving along, is that if a cattleman or a horse breeder calls her, he is usually on hand to wrestle the livestock down for her. Dr. Smith is a diminutive woman who looks a great deal like Mary Martin in the role of Peter Pan.

The Beatles' "Let It Be" was playing on the radio as the three women drove down the two-lane blacktop, chatting with Michigan accents. All wore jeans and boots and jackets. They were going first to see Sarah Varner's Holstein, Sadie, who was down.

In veterinary terms, the cow was carrying a heavy parasite load and a calcium deficiency, which is pretty common this time of year. They have just freshened and they are weak. Dr. Smith had gotten Sadie up a week ago, and had been treating her for pneumonia, but the cow had gotten stuck in the mud and weakened her muscles and she was down again. "The difference between cows and horses going down," Dr. Smith said, "is that a horse will struggle to get up. Call it natural instinct.

"A horse will fight to live. A cow will just lay down and die.

"Jan," Dr. Smith said, sliding out of the car and stepping into the mud, "I need a stethoscope and the thermometer." The tools were fetched from the trunk, and the four of us slogged through a pigsty to the barn. Sadie was on her side in a stall, with hay all around her. Her calf was tied to a post nearby. Dr. Smith inserted a rectal thermometer, then crouched low over the cow to check her heartbeat and to listen for congestion in the lungs. Rain whipped through the stall.

Dr. Smith checked the thermometer and found that the temperature had gone down some. She had last looked in on the cow at eight the night before. She told Jan to get a syringe and some liquid antibiotics from the car, and Jan sloshed off.

"Sadie," Dr. Smith said, waiting on the medication, "I'd like it if you'd just make some attempt to even look like you were going to stand up." The cow didn't even moan.

This year, I was told, shivering there in the stall, has been a bad year for veterinarians as well as cattlemen. The cattlemen haven't felt like paying vet bills, since they are getting so little for their cattle at the market. "They haven't wormed them," Dr. Smith said. "They've just let some of them die. In the long run it may cost them more to get their herds back in shape. . . ."

The medication was administered to Sadie, and Dr. Smith found a note from Sarah Varner. Sarah left the note in the trough. The note said that Homeless, a goat, was in need of attention.

Homeless was tied up two stalls away. (Mrs. Varner names all her animals.) It seems Homeless ate some mountain laurel, which is toxic, a few weeks ago, and Mrs. Varner gave him some mineral oil. Some of the mineral oil got into his lungs, and, eventually, he got pneumonia. Dr. Smith treated him, and now Mrs. Varner thinks he has a cold again. I wrestled with the little white goat, holding it by the horns, then by the neck, trying to still it while Dr. Smith checked temperature, heartbeat and lung congestion. She wound up writing the woman a note, telling her to resume treating it with the antibiotics she already had.

We returned to Sadie the cow, and the four of us pushed and

shoved, trying to get her to turn on her other side, so that her legs would not go to sleep. We were successful, though the cow weighed twice the total weight of the three women. Dr. Smith said they could have accomplished it without me, thank you.

The women and I tracked clumps of mud into the car and headed for a Tennessee walker that needed worming. "I like getting out on the farm and helping people," Dr. Smith said. "I feel like I'm giving more personal service with farm animals than with small pets or that kind of thing."

But Dr. Smith does not turn away pets. As we drove, she told me she recently removed a foot-long spoon from the stomach of a shepherd. The owner had offered the dog a lick, and the dog had swallowed the spoon. She also took two socks from the innards of a Labrador retriever. And a few months ago, the electricity went out while she was amputating a leg on a St. Bernard. She finished the operation on her dining-room table, by flashlight.

She said she decided she would become a veterinarian when she was in the seventh grade. "I can't really say why. It was just something I wanted to do." We talked about her practice in our county, and she said she hopes eventually to get away from this "fire engine" way of running things; emergency calls all day and night. "I would like my practice to be more of a client-education-consultant type operation," she said.

We reached the pasture where the Tennessee walker, called Merry Boy, was quartered. It was raining very hard by then, and it was cold and the women's noses were running. The horse ignored them. He did not want the feed, though four others did. The four practically trampled the women, trying to get to the feed. The women could not lasso Merry Boy.

It was too much; the rain, the cold, the obstinate Tennessee walker. Dr. Smith said she would come back tomorrow, perhaps in the sunshine. She and her helpers drove home to roll bandages on the dining-room table.

The Train

There came a day when I had to go back to work, the full time sort of work that swallows your days and nights, even though you technically owe it only forty hours a week, give or take a lunch. I knew when we decided to move on this farm that if we truly fell in love with what we were doing and where, then I would have to find a way to generate a larger income than we were living on. If we were to stay on this ground, and make it contribute to our sustenance, we would have to work it, not simply walk it and adore it. I recall the scene in the movie *Giant* in which the character Jett Rink inherits land, and he paces off every inch of it in great paces, with the sun going down and silhouetting him and his exaggerated goosesteps. That really is all I had done. A few chickens; a few rabbits (now dead); a small vegetable garden; some repairs on this old farmhouse. A yearling cow was beyond our means. Piglets were twenty dollars at auction each Wednesday. Barbed wire was thirty-six dollars a bale, and today one cannot have livestock unless one has fencing (range laws are still despised by the old people in these mountains). We had been renting and now we were going to buy. Each morning the headlines worsened my economic terror. The job I had left was open, they said, and I took it. Then I stalled for three weeks trying to reckon a way to turn it down.

Once reconciled to work (I am the sort who, like a character I once read about, was genuinely born marked for rest) and to bosses (a year or two ago, I had seen the man who now once more would become my employer poring over a management correspondence lesson entitled: "Should I Socialize with Subordinates?"), the problem at hand became simply how the hell do I get from the farm to the office? It is eighty miles from here to there. The commuting act, we assumed, would be like clawing and scratching to get over a hump.

The alarm clock screamed at five-thirty that first morning, and I got up and stoked the fire and headed for the john. My wife and son were up when I had finished and the boy and I held a race to see who could get dressed first, he winning, by a tennis shoe. We had coffee and cold cereal and none of us said anything. I got up to go and my wife said, "Are you sure you want to do this?" I said, "Are you sure you want to live here?"

"If we're going to live in the city," she said, "we should find a place in the middle of the city. If we're going to live in the country, we should stay here. Screw the suburbs." It was something she had said two years earlier, when we had moved from the heart of a city to its suburb.

We had left a perfectly fine old city house in search of better schools, less crime, a back-yard gardening spot, and cleaner air. We wound up forty minutes away from my office, in a battle zone between a motorcycle lunatic and a screech-voiced crone who did not like the height of my hedges. Our own neighborhood baby-sitters rifled our drawers and stole from us. The helicopter squad of the county police department made a landing pad out of our roof and turned night to day with their searchlights.

Here was where we wanted to be. The task now became how to correlate making a living with living in the country.

We kissed good-by and I went out in the dark. I gave the pony a block of hay and a pail of feed, and I stood there stroking his burr-filled mane while a toenail moon went down behind the ridge. Then I got in the hundred-dollar car and drove. That is

what we have always called this car. My father told me never pay
more than a hundred dollars for a car. That way, he said, if she
goes bad on you, all you got to do is shoot her, or leave her on the
road. Won't hurt a bit, he said. It took me ten years to get over
everybody's automobile mania and assume the ownership of
hundred-dollar cars.

The window on the driver's side is stuck in the down position
on this car. The wind came in hard and cold through the opening
and I shook some as I drove. The town's only traffic light was
blinking yellow on caution when I passed beneath it. The traffic
light does not begin its full three-color duty until 7 A.M. The sun
came up red as I reached the top of Crown Mountain, and everything to the left of me was red, and everything to the right was
black. Jim Hartley, the mayor, who was on the radio, said it might
rain today, and it might not. *Portals of Prayer* came on the radio.
The message this morning concerned selfishness. I did not listen
to it, nor to the *Sundial Sports Report,* nor to the *Sundial Fishing
Report.* I did manage to be content with the sunrise, and the
thought of catching a train for the first time in years and years.

It took twenty minutes to drive to the little green square block
depot in the next town. "She's on time, sir," the clerk said
through the hole in the window. He accepted my two dollars and
ten cents and stamped the ticket. "You should be hearing her any
minute now," he said.

I went through a green swinging door and stood on the platform. The platform began to tremble before the noise came, and
the noise alone, the roar and the deep-throated horn (they call it
a whistle, but no whistle sounds like that) was enough to give a
full-grown man an anticipatory rush.

The first thing I saw was the engine car with the big name
Southern Crescent emblazoned on its great shoulders. The engine
car blurred past, then another engine, then the Desert Palm car,
the Shenandoah River, a freight car, then more with curious
names. Down the line a dozen cars I saw a fat conductor hanging
off the side. He jumped off while the train was slowing, the conductor hitting the ground running, his short, skinny legs trying to

catch up with his balloon body. The conductor all but went into a skid and came to an ungraceful stop just shy of me. "Ticket, sir?" he said, cheeks flushed, sucking wind. I gave it to him.

When the train was dead still and belching, a black porter in a starched white coat swung down from the steps of a passenger car, pulling a black iron stepping stool behind him. He took a white cloth from his hip pocket and he used the cloth to wipe the dust from the brass handrail that runs along the boarding stairs at the rear of the car. He turned to me, took me gently by the elbow, and said, "Watch your step, please, sir." I was the only passenger to board.

There were seven sleeping passengers on this car, which had no sleeping quarters. The wide, thick cushioned seats were arranged in pairs, and the passengers, four men, two women and a child, were curled like dogs on their two-seat berths. The train had come in the night from Washington, D.C.

I heard a loud release of steam and felt a jolt and the train began to move. I saw the porter's reflection in the smoked glass mirror on the wall at the front of the car. He was walking up the aisle behind me with a bundle of newspapers in his arms. "Newspaper, sir?" he whispered. He had a toothbrush mustache, gray, and there were gaps between each of his healthy white teeth. "Breakfast is being served in the dining car," he said. "Just two cars forward."

I took the newspaper, and the suggestion. The dining car was awash in white linen and sterling silver service. A man who bore an astonishing resemblance to Duke Ellington was dining alone. An elderly couple, smartly dressed in the way of the old on Miami Beach, was being served toast and jam, orange juice and coffee. The bright sunlight coming through the tall, wide windows bounced off the silver and the linen and the old man's fashionable wire-rimmed sunglasses and caused me to squint.

"Good morning, sir," the steward said. He was tall and thin and his wrist bones stuck out like marbles. "It looks like you have your choice of tables today." He waved his hand at all the unoccupied tables. I took a seat by a window and directly I was served a mound of scrambled eggs made with cheese, and link sausage, toast, grape jam, and a silver pot of coffee. "Tell me," I said to the steward. "Is it true you still cook with wood stoves on trains?"

"Yes, sir. We do."

"Well, as one who has had trouble keeping firewood all winter, I'd like to know how much you use on board and wherever do you get it?"

"I'll tell you if you won't tell nobody."

"Deal."

"All right, sir. We use Presto logs. You know them pressed sawdust logs they sell for folks' fireplaces? That's them."

I was dashed.

We rolled on through pine forests, the pine straw on the forest floor and on the banks gashed out for the tracks still wet with the morning and glistening in the sun. Occasionally, a small town would burst into view and then be gone. You would catch a glimpse of men loading hay and feed onto the beds of pickup trucks parked outside farmers' exchanges. Occasionally, there would be a big yellow school bus, with red and orange lights flashing all over its front and rear, commanding all to stop while the children boarded. I ate very slowly and thought of my boy and Earl the Pearl, his favorite school bus driver.

We passed a tiny depot in the little town of Chamblee, and someone threw a package off from a freight car up ahead. The package landed at the feet of a man on the depot platform, and the man made a sign like an umpire does in baseball when a runner is called safe at base.

I poured myself another cup of coffee as we crossed over the city's interstate beltway, the highway strangled with cars, none moving, some honking. We passed through a district of mansions and I saw a man in a blue cardigan sweater and a white golf shirt, taking his breakfast on his second-story back porch, wave at the engineer, an act he probably does daily.

And we were there, at the station, stopped, the train emitting bursts of steam like bullets. "Watch your step, sir," the porter

said, guiding me lightly by the elbow. The train pulled out for
New Orleans. It would be foolish to think that it would always go
this smoothly, but, damn, wasn't that fine?

Postscript: I did not stay with the job very long. Just long
enough to pay for a new front porch, and new windows, and
eleven gallons of paint. And salt a little money away. It does not
take very much to live, we decided. And besides, I hate jobs. As
long as I can get along without one, I will. Simple theory, easily
practiced.

Running

It has been months since I was in good shape physically. (It has been twenty years since I was on balance in the other department, but that isn't the subject today.) Shamelessly, I've let myself grow and soften, eating whatever and whenever, staying up all hours of the night, moving from cushion to cushion to bed. In this house, we do not have a single mirror which affords a view of one's whole self. Shaving every third or fourth day, I was pleased to find that my head and neck sizes appeared stable, and as for the rest of me, well, from up here things looked pretty good. Health alarms sounded on the occasion of the purchase of a new pair of britches. "Let me see," the store clerk said, "you look to me to be about a thirty-five." "Thirty-three," I said. This morning, I set out to run.

You have here no stranger to the long-distance foot flight. In the city I belonged to a club, a health club that employed blind masseurs who stepped on my bare toes while making their ways about. I ran three miles of sidewalk in the late afternoons, along the route passing car after backed up car caught in the daily traffic jam, and it was only after I began to feel that I would die from carbon monoxide that I gave it up. Hung up the jockstrap and returned to a comfortable, and slovenly, lifestyle.

"What are you doing in there?"

"I'm looking for my jogging shorts."

"It sounds like you're tearing up the whole bedroom."

"Where are my jogging shorts?"

"Your what?"

"The shorts I used to run in."

"Oh. I've been using them for a dustcloth."

Clad in tee-shirt, deep purple paisley Bermudas, sweat socks and tennis shoes, I did my limbering exercises in the living room.

"Hey, Mom. What's he doing?"

"He's going to run."

"Run?"

"That's what he says."

"Run where, Dad?"

"To Marge's store. Umph." Eighteen sit-ups. Nineteen sit-ups. Twenty sit-ups. "And back."

"Wow! I've got to *see* this."

It was decided that he would ride his pony to the store and wait for me there. I did not want an entourage on this first outing. I already felt, and looked, ridiculous. He went to the barn, saddled up, and struck out, calling back that he would wait for me at the gas pumps. Now I was outside, doing knee bends. Ahead lay one mile of dirt and in that mile two difficult hills and at the end of that mile Marge's store.

Hi-Yo Fat Man, Awaaaaaay!

Left at the mailbox and onto the road. An absolutely perfect morning for running, if there is such a thing. Mist in the high meadow, mist in the bog. Buds on the dogwoods and blooms on the azaleas. Airy April cirrus to the north and unblemished blue to the south. I smell cow manure and I smell bacon frying. Now approaching, now beneath, now beyond the great white oak that leans over the road and looks today as it has always looked: it will crash down any second. Past the long, gray, squatty chicken house on the right. On the left a milk cow, her udder so full that the

teats hang in the dark green fescue. Everywhere, the sound of trac-
tors. It is the season's first dry day and everyone is plowing. There
goes Mr. Gilstrap down the two-rut trail that runs around the base
of John Jones Mountain, Mr. Gilstrap sitting tall and straight
atop his machine. Morning, Mr. Lingerfelt. Morning, Mrs. Sammons. Mrs. Sammons has sheets and pillowcases hanging on the
line. Up, up and over the first hill. Wind holding out, legs still
good. There is a dog pack at my heels. I look over my shoulder and
closest to me is Jerry, a poodle, our poodle, object of my enmity,
and behind Jerry is Bert, a bitch, our bitch, who is in heat, and
who is followed by Sherman, a redbone from up the road, and
Sherman seems intent on mounting Bert, and behind Sherman is
Gladys, a blue tick, who, when her time comes, will be diddled by
Sherman too, and joining all of them are a black shepherd and a
Chihuahua, both loosely owned by Mrs. Sammons, and coming
lickety-split on the tail of this aggregation, this United Nations assembly of the canine world, is a St. Bernard owned by the county
ordinary, and up ahead, in the middle of the road, is a big black
bull with the pinkeye. I stop.

The bull, standing broadside to me and my mob, appears more
curious than annoyed. He makes no sound. All the male dogs at
my rear are growling and gnawing at one another—all save one,
Sherman, who is having a fine time with my bitch Bert, who gives
of herself freely. It is vaudeville. I slip off the right of the road,
over an electric cattle wire, over a downed sweet gum covered with
mushrooms, behind yet another chicken house, through a pasture
rich in manure and phlox, poor in daffodils, down by the creek
the kids skinnydip in, the creek cold and green this morning, and
back to the road beyond the second hill, out of sight of the me-
nagerie. I have not been followed. I still hear the dogs.

There is nothing arduous about the last tenth mile of the run
and I take it without sweat. The pony is tied to the premium
pump. The boy sits on a soft drink case, drinking a grape drink.
"Sure took you a long time."

"I had to detour. All the dogs followed me. And there's a bull
in the road."

"That old bull is always out. He won't hurt you. Want me to ride back? All the dogs'll follow me."

"Please."

He leaves me with a quarter to buy myself a drink and I go in the store to suffer one last indignity. There is a huge sheet of cardboard on the wall above the cash register and written on the top of it is the word MISTRUSTED. And below MISTRUSTED are the names of the louts who have written bad checks at this establishment. My wife told me we had erred in this manner and that she had corrected it immediately. Yet, there, third name from the top, is me. A line had been drawn through the lettering with a tiny, hard-leaded pencil, apparently to show we had made good our mistake. Nevertheless, the name would stay there, clearly legible, for all the world to see, for the life of the cardboard. I back out the door, unspotted so far, mortified man in purple paisley. There is no one and no thing on the road as I walk it home.

Idiot Eastward Bound

There is a certain flat sameness to most adults' days, and when I feel it in mine, when I grow bored, I try to change. I scheme. I come up with plans that could be called harebrained. To get right to it: Tomorrow I leave on a bicycle in an attempt to pedal from the mountains to the sea. That, then, is that.

It has been years since I have ridden a bicycle any distance. But I am well outfitted. I have obtained a rakish, ten-speed model of craftsmanship. It bears absolutely no resemblance to the last bike that was mine. In those days, Schwinn was status, and I had a Schwinn, a bile-green beauty with two great springs on the front fork to cushion the ride. The old man liked it too, and he rode it backwards one freewheeling New Year's Eve, hit a parked car, wound up in an uncomfortable sprawl atop a Winged Victory hood ornament. Bent the rim and broke nine spokes.

I painted it a hot, hot red with a brush one spring and rode it over to a girl's house. "Thing of beauty," she said, or I imagined, and she rode the crossbar between me and the handlebars. Kissed me. The white shorts she wore that day would forever sport a single red stripe across the rear.

Loved that bike. Mistreated it. Kept it out in the rain. Left it out in the front yard and somebody stole it. Twenty years later I find myself in possession of a fine English model, weighing

twenty-four pounds, color white with blue trim, specially made for touring. I also have a lightweight tent, a lightweight sleeping bag, and a change of clothing.

Tomorrow, the road.

Out of the hills of Habersham on Highway 17! No clouds. No traffic. A dead possum flat as a sail here and there. And a grade going down, down, down. It is so steep you cannot pedal, even in the highest gear. Tears form at the outside corners of the eyes, streak back along the temples and are lost in the wind. The back is parallel to the bicycle, the chin jutted out front of the handlebars. Anything for a speedometer at this moment. How fast? the mind wonders. How much faster?

The road was laid in twelve-foot sections of concrete and the cracks were sealed with asphalt. The stingy, spoked wheels are going whap-whap-whap as they hit the cracks. The whap sounds are coming so close together that bike and rider must surely be exceeding the speed limit.

We are at hill's bottom and streaking upward. Wings could have put us in the pine tree tops. What a rush!

The exhilaration is done. It is terribly tough, this making it to the top of the next grade. Fifth gear. Fourth gear. Third. Second. First. Walk. That is the way it has been all day. With each hill, you exhaust yourself on its front, excite yourself on its back.

My wife and daughter let me out this morning on a county road at the top of a mountain. We played a sort of leapfrog for a while. My wife would roar past and I would wave and my daughter would wave and I would think, "Well, they're gone." Then I would round a bend and there they would be, my wife taking pictures, my girl jumping up and down. I wished for a long time after they stopped doing this that they would reappear somewhere down the road.

Near night, I stopped at two farmhouses several miles outside a small town and asked if I could pitch my tent. I had visions of a beauty in calico, her long honey-hair done back in a dairy maid's bun, saying, "Newt's out milking, but I'm sure he wouldn't mind putting you up in the barn. Would you have some supper with us?"

"Wouldn't want to be a bother, ma'am."

"No bother. We got some homemade peach ice cream left over from Sunday."

"Could you show me where I could knock some of this trail dust off me, ma'am?"

But the old women at both farmhouses looked at me as they would a mother-stabber, and grunted there was a roadside park two-three miles yonder. The park, just above the town waterworks, had three picnic tables and no flat ground, save the parking lot. At considerable difficulty, the tent was pitched and pegged at a slant. I had nothing to eat. I slept the thick sleep of the weary.

Frank Hooper called my name at seven on this, the third morning of my journey. I was already awake. The crows had been screaming since six. "Hey," Frank yelled, "get up. I got the catfish stew warming."

There was a cool wind coming off the Savannah River, which is broad, flat and green at this point, and the drone of a small motor could be heard from way far away. Someone was running trot lines. The flaps were up on the tent, and the wind brought in the smell of onions in the catfish stew. It was loaded with onions.

I walked down to the river to stretch and yawn, and when I got back Frank had breakfast ready. He had heated the stew and grits and tea. His tent was pitched about thirty-five yards from mine. He has lived in it a year.

Frank Hooper teaches science at the Middle School across the river in Calhoun Falls, a textile mill town. He came up, stuck out his hand and shook mine when I rolled into this camping area last night, at the end of a very long day.

There had been the little town of Bowman, where Mr. and Mrs. Woodrow Lavender were at work landscaping the square. Mr. Lavender is the city attorney, though you could not tell it from his appearance. He wore green overalls and carried a spade. He had a huge wad of tobacco in his mouth. Mrs. Lavender, a stout woman, had a scarf on her head. They were planting Vinca Minor, a ground cover that grows well in the shade. Ten old water oaks shade the square and the foot traffic and the rain have kept the ground sloppy.

They were also planting zoysia grass and they had set out dogwoods and some rotunda holly and some dwarf Buford holly. Mrs. Lavender regretted that she had forgotten to get azaleas, for her back yard is full of them.

There is a town well at one end of the square and it is covered with a shelter that has an octagonal roof. Strings of Christmas lights are affixed to the shelter. There are four benches under the shelter, and elderly gentlemen pass time there.

"They sat there all day yesterday and watched us dig up this ground and the only one offered to help us was J. E. Gaines, him with his false leg," Mrs. Lavender said.

I stayed just long enough to have a Coke, heavy with syrup, from the corner drugstore, and then I pedaled on down Highway 17, its shoulders covered with crimson clover and crape myrtle.

Earlier I had been in the town of Royston, which lays claim to Ty Cobb, a famous base stealer. There is a Ty Cobb museum there. There is no old uniform, no cleats, no bat that he ever really used in the Ty Cobb Museum. Just pictures, clippings and trophies. It is a large block building, housing little more than a grade school exhibit. The curator was not there, and the yardman said, "Sure, sure." Inside was very quiet. There was only the sound of the water cooler.

Later in the day I got beaned with some loose rocks from a gravel truck on an overpass outside the town of Elberton. One knot is plumped out the size of a quarter.

At sundown came this park and Frank Hooper, who invited me for supper. He had some chili that his wife had made and a head of lettuce and some kind of green salad dressing with garlic in it. He said he had been living here by the river, Monday through Friday, since last spring. His wife and five children live seventy-five miles away in a town called Greer, where she teaches school.

Frank has long, curly black hair and a round friendly face and he wears black, horn-rimmed glasses. You can tell he is not the best-equipped camper in the world. He had to search a long time for a spoon, and finally settled for a fork. He found two plastic bowls and a pot in some dark corner of his tent. Then he announced he was ready to cook.

We drank whisky out of paper cups while the chili was heating and Frank talked about the ten years he and his family spent in Israel when he was with the Baptist ministry. He had a falling out with religion because his church refused to change, refused to accept anything new, he said.

We tore at the lettuce and put it in the bowl. We covered it with salad dressing. When the chili was hot, we floored the bowls with more lettuce and poured the chili over it. The chili was ground beef and kidney beans and tomatoes.

After supper, Frank admired my bike and said he was just helping his oldest boy buy the same model. There is a canoe near Frank's tent. His oldest boy built it of pine wood and canvas.

We talked until ten, when Frank said he had to go to a pay telephone down the road and call his wife. This morning when we had finished the catfish stew, and I was washing the dishes, and Frank was leaving for school, I asked him if he had reached his wife.

"Yeah," he said. "It's kinda sad. You know that bike I was telling you about? Somebody stole it. My boy will take that hard."

After Frank left I decided not to ride because I thought it was going to rain. It did not rain. Two other things I did not do were fish and read. I started to read, but found that the only book I brought was a complete guide to trees west of the Rocky Mountains.

So I sat down by the Savannah River on a big old log that had washed up and the sun had bleached white. Small fishing craft pushed along by small Evinrude and Mercury motors were all over the river. And in every single boat there were couples who looked like they had been married for a long, long time. Many of the women wore wide-brimmed straw hats and many of the men wore long-billed caps. They were fishing for bass and bream and crappie and they were having very bad luck in the morning. But they were happy to be together, you could tell that.

"Sam!" the woman hollered as they passed my point. I could hear her well above the boat motor. Sam, who may or may not have been dozing in the stern, snapped to and took off his cap and wiped his forehead with his forearm.

"If you don't start paying attention to driving this boat, I want to be taken right back!"

"Aw, honey."

"I mean it."

"Aw, honey."

"Sam . . ."

And they were gone.

After a while I went to sleep and the sound of the brown water lapping there against the banks, and the wind in the pines and the poplars, made it a deep, dreamless sleep. The soreness was there again when I woke. The soreness is there every morning, particularly in the hindquarters. It is like the drinker grown accustomed to the hangover. Without the hangover, he would wake knowing he was feeling as good as he would feel all day. So it is with the soreness. The soreness has been with me twice today.

Clyde Webb just dropped by my campsite to show me his scrapbook. Clyde is a retired carpenter who keeps everything tidy around here and his scrapbook is filled with color snapshots of him and great strings of fish. And him and campers' children. And him and campers and children and fish. The children are always stealing cubes out of the bags of ice that Clyde sells for fifty cents. Clyde lets them take the ice and says nothing.

There is a letter in the scrapbook from a Florida woman who camped here last year with her family. The letter is addressed to the director of natural resources for the state. She writes: "God made a special man when He made Clyde; He picked up assorted pieces just as He did for all of us, but when He put them together in him, He added a little something extra—thoughtfulness, kindness, humility, graciousness—Clyde has them all."

Clyde, who is slight and gray and talks very loud, built a building and gave it to the park. They use it for cookouts and group meetings. He built a fireplace, but had to tear it down the first time. It wouldn't draw. "She'll pull now," Clyde said. "She'll pull now." Above the hearth there is a plaque that says Clyde's Shed.

Most all the people in public campgrounds during the week are old. They are retired and they are fishing through a piece of the world. Theo Harris is doing this. Theo Harris is a retired mailman who sat with me while I tightened everything on the bike this afternoon. He told me he and his wife took a three-and-a-half-month camping trip to Alaska not long ago. He said he covered seventeen thousand miles on that trip, and the one thing he remembers about Alaska is that the mosquitoes nearly carried him away. He went to slay the great fish, but when he got there he found that you had to get way back in the wilderness to land the big ones, and he didn't go back in far enough. Nevertheless, he said, it was an enjoyable trip. So was the one to Nova Scotia. So will be the one next week, though he doesn't know where that will be yet. One thing for sure, he said, he won't stay home and grow daft.

Theo Harris and Clyde Webb stopped back by after dark and sat around the fire with me. Theo looks like everybody's mental image of a postman. Tall, gaunt, gray-haired, with tiny wire-rimmed glasses and a white mustache. I watched the flames dance on the lenses of both men's glasses. They both wore sweaters because it was cold.

Theo said television is what is wrong with the world today. "People stare at that box for hours on end and they don't even pay no mind to what's on," Theo said. And Clyde said we are rapidly returning to heathenism and that all will be lost unless we get back to God. They left about nine and I stayed by the fire until it was gone.

The weekend had some dark shades. There was Friday night in a state park on a patch of gravel, smaller than a driveway, in my tent between an Eleganza Mark Custom A1A Super something and a Scout Chief Thunder Over Under Van for All Seasons. Our driveway was just across a flat brown stretch of water from the ramp, down which more than a hundred cars backed and deposited fiberglass boats with bows shaped like shovels.

There is a no-sweat technique to getting a boat off its trailer and into the water and, watching there from our driveway (my wife and children had joined me for the weekend), we had front row seats to an evening human comedy. Those with the proper touch would first disengage the cable that holds boat to trailer. Then they would back fast until the car's rear wheels were in water. Then they would shove the car into a forward gear and hightail it up the ramp. This maneuver will thrust the boat onto the water with no effort on anyone's part but the driver's.

For every boat deposited deftly, we saw a dozen struggles. The old man would back gently to water's edge, then the old lady would get out and, trying hard not to get her feet wet, she would disengage the cable and put shoulder to bow and push. "Won't budge," we heard time after time. "Should I back up more?" "No, no. It's up to my knees now." Then driver and shover would switch roles and the scene would go on and on and on, only to be replayed by other boaters as soon as their predecessors were successful and got the hell out of the way.

We threw two cans of vegetable soup into a skillet with hamburger meat and onions, ate, slept, paid our three dollars and split. I put the bicycle in the back and my wife drove and I got a forty-mile free ride, no pedaling, all the way to Augusta, where an appointment had been made with a master bike mechanic who would correct all the damage I had wrought during the journey from the mountains.

We killed time by diving for pennies at the bottom of a concrete swimming pool beneath a tall bank billboard, the billboard
effectively shading the pool. The pool belonged to a motel that accepted our fourteen dollars in return for a room in which the
heater worked fine and would not shut off, though it was toasty
outside during the night. We dived for our own pennies in a pool
that lay next to the Fort Gordon Highway and was surrounded
by, from left to right, Valentine Used Cars—We Finance—Good
or Bad Credit; South American—the Guaranteed Car Service; Tal-
madge Lewis Motors; H & S Transfer Co., Inc.; GMC Used Truck
Center; Garden City Package Shop; Kirby Cycles; Key Wholesale
—Everybody Welcome; Garden City Bowl; and Howard Johnson's.

We took pleasure in being together and laughed at what we
were doing and where, and wondered whether anyone ever had
fun at an execution. We caught up on all the news from home
and said our good-bys on Sunday morning and I pedaled south on
Highway 56, feeling like the whole world was in church. And
someone ought to take time this spring to clear out some of the
honeysuckle along here because the smell is overpowering.

The wind created small dust whirlwinds in the parking lot of
the Piney Grove Baptist Church, and I stopped there long enough
to hear a baby cry, and two authoritative coughs. Above it all,
there was the message that now is the time new seeds hit the
ground and new seeds of kindness ought to hit the heart.

I am getting so good with this pedaling, and this fine bike and I
have become such a co-operative, that it is my fancy to one day
pass a truck. Having done that, I will retire the derailleur system
and hang it on the wall above the hearth. This was the thought I
was having as country music struck my ears as I was rounding a
curve and coming into Waynesboro, a town of 6,500.

The music was coming from the grand opening of Waynesboro's first big-time apartment complex. "We have some of your
housing authority units," a host explained, "but this is the first
real apartment complex for Waynesboro." The apartments, called

Briarwood, are in two-story brick buildings set on a treeless pasture. It seemed the entire staff of radio station WBRO was there broadcasting live from beneath a huge floral umbrella. It was hot, but not as hot as one day last fall when they were broadcasting live from the Farm Service Center and the sun warped all the phonograph records, I was told.

Doris Lewis, the station manager, a woman of healthy construction wearing white pants and white, stacked-heel sandals and a black, sleeveless turtleneck blouse and black hair and sunglasses, worried with all the particulars and ordered her employes to synchronize their watches with the station clock because she wanted it "on the nose" when they went on the air at two.

Among the employes were Bob Black, who ran the black console control board beneath the umbrella and who is engaged to be married to Doris Lewis. Bob Black, who has a profile similar to the Indian side of the buffalo nickel, was in a good mood, considering. The man who lives in the corner house across the highway had been over to complain about the music. Black had set out two speakers next to the highway. The man had said his wife was trying to sleep. Black turned down the volume on Boots Randolph, who was playing "Once a Day, Every Day, All Day Long" on his saxophone. "Anybody cain't sleep with that kind of music," Black said, "ain't got no business sleeping."

Directly, Tom Cooper showed up. Cooper was to be the deejay on the live broadcast from the Briarwood Apartments. He wore a cranberry-colored shirt and tie and pants and brown, pointed-toe cowboy boots polished highly and a belt with a silver buckle that had cattle brands and a chuck wagon on it. Everybody knew Tom and most of the women came up and hugged him. One woman came up and hugged him and Tom said, "Old J.C. got all right, didn't he?"

"Darn it," the woman said.

"They gonna git you," Tom told her.

Just before broadcast time there was some difficulty in locating the list of door prizes. There were to be eighteen, only the woman in charge of the prizes could only remember fifteen, including ten

pounds of T-bone steak and a case of motor oil. A man named
Rufus was dispatched to put the legs on the barbecue grill, the
grand prize. And Doris Lewis told Tom Cooper not to announce
the prizes from the three furniture companies all in a row because
they are in direct competition with one another.

As she was saying that, Doris Lewis put her book down on the
control board. Her book was in a crimson plastic book cover that
made it look like a Bible. It was *The Wildest Heart,* and it concerned "Desire, Love & Passion," according to the first page. Bob
Black, who was running the control board, told Doris Lewis,
"Woman, stop putting that book in my face. I ain't got room
enough here now to cuss a cat without getting a hair in my
mouth!"

At two o'clock, they kicked off the show with Billie Jo Spears
singing "Blanket on the Ground." Tom signed on with: "And a
pleasant good afternoon to you, neighbors. Tom Cooper here feeling good like I know I should on a Cooper afternoon. We're out
here at the grand opening of the Briarwood Apartments . . ."
After the record ended, Tom told his listening audience, "Ah yes,
sugar booger!"

Doris Lewis walked back from the highway and said, "Tom, we
got to get some people off that road. They're expecting a thousand."

"Well, Doris, we just started," Tom said.

Then there was some discussion over whether to give away the
RCs by the case or by the carton. Doris Lewis said, "We could
drag it out longer if we gave them away by the carton."

And I rode on to a good restaurant where a state patrolman
impressed the two young waitresses with his cigarette lighter,
which could produce a flame big as a bonfire or small as a pin-
point.

Now in the flatland and nearing the coast. It had been a hot,
dull day, livened only by an occasional fast dog, and there were
dead things all along the road. Tire after tire had ironed the dead
things. There were six dead rattlesnakes and four dead bullfrogs,

three dead possums and one dead cat. There were three fat healthy rattlesnakes, too. That was lively.

Five miles outside the town of Sylvania there was a sandy road leading off to the right and there was a sign saying it led to the Seaborn Goodall home, which was built in 1815. But the wind had blown a great old water oak across the road and you couldn't get through to the house. I didn't know about the curse that sacked the town that used to surround the house. I just thought I'd leave it be and come back another time.

Everything is kind of hurting along here. When they built the Interstate Highway, it took a lot of traffic off this road. The motels are hurting the most. One has closed. They also built a highway loop around Sylvania. That hurt the downtown. A barber named Jesse Blakey told me the loop was just another in a long stretch of hurts for him. "Long hair cut us in half," Jesse said. "Recession cut us twenty per cent. We're down to the bone."

To get to downtown, you turn off the loop onto Main Street and you pass stately houses, some with columns and some with splendid manicured lawns. First there is the house of the secretary-treasurer of the bank, then the undertaker's house; the dentist's; the retired druggist's; the bank president's; the bank vice-president's; the house of the oldest licensed realtor in the county; the president of the other bank; the owner of Minkovitz Department Store; the nigger house; the Methodist parsonage; and the mansion, which is part of the estate of the late Nellie Morrell Hill. Yes, the nigger house. That is what everyone calls it. Apparently, that is what it is called.

The First Methodist Church is on one end of the business district and the First Baptist Church is on the other. Jesse Blakey's barbershop is exactly halfway between the churches. He has four chairs in his shop, though there is only Jesse and his partner, James Rooks. James Rooks used to have four chairs, and four barbers, in his shop across the street. James Rooks' four chairs are in the back of Jesse Blakey's shop. The chairs are dusty.

"We need us a bill like the dentists and the doctors have," Jesse said to James while I was there. "People need to be able to get a shave or a haircut with Medicare or food stamps or something. Look at me. Here it is two minutes to two and I've had two customers all day. Prosperity. You can't beat it."

It was Jesse who told me about the Seaborn Goodall House and the curse. He put me in touch with a Mrs. Bowey, who called Essie Hollingsworth and asked her to drive me out there. Quickly, the curse: In the early nineteenth century, Jacksonboro was the seat of this county, which is called Screven. Sylvania did not exist. Seaborn was the clerk of the Superior Court and his home was the best in Jacksonboro. The town was mean as a snake and lawless and its lumbermen drank and fought and generally good-timed themselves to death. Essie Hollingsworth remembers reading this of Jacksonboro: "It was reported that in the mornings after drunken frolics and fights you could see the children picking up eyeballs in tea saucers."

In strode an itinerant, eccentric, hunchbacked preacher named Lorenza Dow. With the exception of Seaborn Goodall, the whole town came down hard on Lorenza and his meddling. Seaborn washed Lorenza's wounds and gave him a place to stay. Next day, Lorenza was rotten-egged out of Jacksonboro. Lorenza got safely across Beaver Dam Creek, knocked his feet together to get the dust off, and pronounced a curse on Jacksonboro. All but the Goodall home would go, according to Lorenza Dow.

There is no evidence today that there ever was a Jacksonboro. Searchers have found neither nail nor plank nor chimney stone. Only the Seaborn Goodall home remains.

Essie Hollingsworth and the other ladies of the Daughters of the American Revolution are raising money to have the Goodall House restored. Mrs. Hollingsworth picked me up in her car and we stopped by the First Methodist Church to pick up Elizabeth Lee, who is a church secretary and who knows much about the house.

"I'll be right with you, Essie," Elizabeth yelled from the church porch. "They're recording a Dial-a-Prayer inside and I have to wait to get my purse." She said later, after she was in the car, that the regular minister was away and the young minister was nervous about recording his first Dial-a-Prayer. "So we went out of the room while he did it," Elizabeth said.

We passed a live rattlesnake and a rat snake and a dead rattlesnake on the road and went down a back road to the Goodall House. The house has two stories, a large front porch and three chimneys. It sits just to the rear of an old moss-covered catalpa tree and to the rear of the house is a trailer. Ophie Gardner lives in the trailer. He is rebuilding the house.

Ophie had to replace most of the weather boarding. It was too rotten to nail to. The house now has a new cypress shingle roof. The carpenter and I talked while Miss Lee and Mrs. Hollingsworth inspected the work.

"It was a craftsman that designed it," Ophie said. "No doubt about that. But slaves did the work."

The walls were built elsewhere, probably beneath a shed in the fall when there was little other work to do. Then they were brought to the site and fitted into place like a jigsaw puzzle. All the important timbers have Roman numerals notched in them. The slaves had to hew the massive twelve-by-fourteen cypress sills beneath the house, and everything else, for that matter. The house was built on what the carpenter calls the principle of six. Six support piers beneath it and six huge timbers, three in front and three in back, from which everything is framed. Heart pine pegs and nails fashioned by a blacksmith hold the house together.

Miss Lee and Mrs. Hollingsworth were having a discussion outside. "Elizabeth, they want us to decide whether we want the bannisters green to match the blinds or not."

"I guess we have to do some research."

"Well, they painted them green originally."

"Did?"

"Yes."

"Then I guess we should."

Ophie Gardner was talking about the 160-year-old bricks in the chimney. He is a short fat man with red cheeks and he wore a small gray cap with a stingy bill. "Oh yes," he said. "I love my work. You can't build something back unless you have a feeling for it." Then he talked about how the house was so out of plumb from a hurricane that came through sixty years ago.

On the ride back to town, we talked about blackberry jam and what a wonderful find Ophie Gardner was and how the women need more donations if they are going to get the house back in first-class shape. They have already spent $15,000 on it. I had one last cup of coffee with the barber, Jesse Blakey, before leaving town and he talked about money too.

"We got a philosophy around here that the poor man's like the honeybee," Jesse said. "If you don't rob him, he won't work."

And so there it was, Savannah, the welcome end to a long haul. Ten days and four hundred twenty miles. Visions of hot baths and great meals, soft music and cool drinks danced in the brain, the brain addlepated, baked by the sun. One approaching thought: This old bike must think it queer to stop without a farmhouse near. That's how bad off the brain was.

Thanks to my wife, there was money waiting at the Western Union office and there was a reservation at the Desoto Hilton. Because of the trucks, the last twenty miles had been treacherous and not at all worth the effort. But in downtown Savannah, the motorists give you wide range, and you can pedal without fear round the old squares.

"Service!" There the voice of the desk clerk. The bellman took the bicycle by the handlebars and rolled it to the elevator. It must have looked odd, for many people stared. The bellman rolling the bike, the bike making its well-engineered tick-tick-tick sound, and the biker following behind, grinning, sunburned, stinking bad as an overflowed septic tank.

It was very cold in the room. Too, the room had cool, floral colors. Along the way, there had been three motel rooms that were never cool. The temperature had been controlled by the management. The management had also controlled the hot water. There was never any hot water.

One must play this Savannah situation right. First, lay in the proper supplies. There was a fine men's clothing shop four blocks away, and it yielded a shirt of pima cotton, light and airy, and a pair of undershorts, a pair of socks, and a comb. The drugstore sold me a bottle of shampoo, an expensive bar of soap, and nail clippers. The liquor store with the cuted up façade, a half pint of good scotch whisky.

Now fill the tub with warm water, pour the drink over the ice, and place the glass on the sideboard, in easy reach of the bath. Now into the bath and just sit there, letting the water cool, and when it cools, all you have to do is let it drain, and refill it. Recollections of the trip came easy.

The poor black families on the porches of their shacks in the lowland. "Helloooo, there!" I yelled from the bike. "Fine. Fine." That was always the reply. "Fine. Just fine."

A man named Fletcher Sanders, who works on small motors. Standing there in his store when the preacher came in. Fletcher's wife runs the store and he does his mechanicking outside. "Fellow told me he'd like to have your job," Fletcher told the preacher. "I told him I wouldn't have your job for nuthin' in the world. Always on the road. Preachin' here. Preachin' there. Preachin's a hard life. Take me, I'd ruther work on lawn mowers."

All those fast hungry yard dogs.

Now out of the tub and toweled and sitting on the balcony in my shorts, sipping. There is a pool party going on below. All the women are in evening gowns and the men are in dinner jackets. The food is on warmers, and the bar is at one end of the pool, and a four-piece combo is playing at the other end. The lady singer with the silver hair is singing "Puppy Love" and "As Time Goes By," "Cry Me a River" and "My Funny Valentine," "Mack the Knife" and "Up a Lazy River." There is a cool south wind and the women in the gowns with spaghetti straps are dancing very close to their partners.

It is only six blocks to the Olde Pink House, a good restaurant a pleasant walk away. I take a cab, hedonist to the marrow. Get a table by the window. Look out on the square. Start with black turtle bean soup. Then the salad, the salad covered with marinated chick-peas. The City Cafe in Lavonia had been nice, with its meat loaf and fresh corn, mashed potatoes and green beans, hot rolls and corn bread, all for a dollar and something. This meal would cost fifteen times the other, and well worth it.

A young couple, just married last Saturday in St. Louis, occupies the next table. They have been to Louisville, Gatlinburg, today Savannah, tomorrow Orlando. I tell them they ought to slow up, stay awhile. Why? they ask. There are places to go, things to see. They have steaks. I have baby flounder, stuffed with crab meat. And a half bottle of a decent white wine. The entree comes with something the restaurant calls its secret vegetable. It isn't very secret tonight. It is a rutabaga heart, fried in batter.

Coffee and brandy. A long, leisurely walk back to the hotel, through the squares, looking at the monuments, hearing the wind in the water oaks. The linen on the bed smells perfumed. Not a heavy perfume. A light, quite pleasant smell.

Home, tomorrow, by airplane. Sometimes a man has to do something cockeyed in order to hold on. Or something like that.

Plowing

Dillard Gilstrap, a man I would like to have as grandfather if that role were not filled, was plowing in the high meadow this morning. The noise from his tractor engine woke us all, and I took my coffee to the front porch and sat there a long time watching him labor. This meadow he was plowing is beyond the road, the low meadow, the branch, and a stand of poplars and willows; it is a good distance from the porch and I could hear him more than I could see him. The tractor, a recently painted high red, would come in view briefly, its driver sitting straight as he would in a ladder-back chair, and then be lost to sight. Mr. Gilstrap is plowing our property, with our permission.

A few nights ago, Nancy Gilstrap, a daughter-in-law of the old man, called to ask if they could lease some of our land for the spring and summer. This resulted in a four-way conversation because her husband, Claude, the eldest son of Dillard Gilstrap, must surely hate the telephone as much as I. Here is the way it went, with Nancy Gilstrap and my wife on the phone, and Claude Gilstrap and me yelling to our wives from our respective living rooms:

"Nancy says Claude wants to know if he can use some of our land to plant. Greg! [Yelling from the bedroom now.] Do you hear me?"

"Huh?"

"Nancy says Claude wants to know if he can plant some of our land."

"Ask her how much he wants to pay."

"Nancy, Greg wants to know how much he usually pays."

There was a great pause here, while Nancy hollered to Claude and Claude hollered his response. Then Nancy told my wife and my wife told me, "Nancy says Claude says they never have paid money. They fertilize it heavily and it's good for the land, and he'll give us all the vegetables we could use. That's what they usually pay."

I said, "Tell her to tell him I guesso."

She did, and that was that. Two days later, Dillard Gilstrap, father of Claude, came down (all the Gilstraps live a half mile up the dirt road) and gave us fifteen white leghorns, a payment we did not expect. The hens took twenty-four hours to become accustomed to new surroundings, then began laying. To me, this whole transaction, the promise of fertilizer, vegetables, and now these chickens, seems a very fine manner in which to fork over the rent. I couldn't be happier. And so it was with pleasure I awoke to the sound of the old man plowing today.

Mr. Gilstrap plowed in a circle, beginning at the far edges of the meadow, and getting closer with each lap to the single dead apple tree in the middle of what would become his new cornfield. It was good to see the high yellow broom sedge (a sign of poor soil, some say) disappear behind the tractor and be replaced with an ever-widening circle of dark red earth. It was as pleasing to the eye as watching a fresh coat of white paint cover the dingy, grease-spattered walls of a kitchen. It was disappointing to hear the tractor cough dead in midmorning, seeing the field only half plowed. It seemed necessary to find the cause of this interruption.

Dillard Gilstrap sat on the ground on the lower corner of the meadow, his tractor parked before him. I have come to know him as a spry, unhurried gentleman who was born in the last century.

He sat smoking his pipe with his legs stretched out front of him, his ankles crossed, and his hands palms down on the ground back of him. The sweat drops had run down his face and gathered in his white whiskers. His greeting was, "Have your breakfast?" Told yes, he said, "Some folks think bacon and eggs is the finest breakfast in the world."

Asked what he himself had for breakfast, Mr. Gilstrap shut his eyelids and smiled, as if the thought gave him tremendous pleasure. "I always have," he said, then lost the thought. He tried to pick it up again. "I *always* have . . ." His eyes opened and his forehead wrinkled and he said, "It'll come to me! It'll come to me!" But it never did.

Claude Gilstrap walked onto the scene a few minutes later. Claude is a man of considerable energy. He works seventy miles away in a General Motors plant, and comes home each evening to see after no end of farming chores. He and his father raise hogs, cattle (this field of mine will be planted in corn for feed for their livestock) and every crop the region will grow. Claude has black hair, the slight frame of his father, and blue eyes that never gaze directly at yours. "Taking a break, Daddy?" Claude asked.

The old man leaned back so that his face caught full sun, and he said, "Yep. Yep. Taking a break."

"Well, Daddy," Claude said, "I meant to get back sooner. But you know how those funerals go. Sometimes they go on and on. And I had to go, you know, being a pallbearer."

"Yep. Yep," the old man said.

"Well, Daddy," Claude said, patting the big mud tire on the tractor, "I think I'll take her around a time or two. Think I'll lay some down. Did you check the oil?"

"Yep. Yep," the old man said. "She's got plenty oil."

"Think I'll check it to be sure," Claude said. He pulled the dipstick, wiped it on his khaki pants, replaced it and pulled it again. "Plenty oil," Claude said. "Well, think I'll take her around a time or two."

"You won't get very far," the old man said. He leaned back and cupped his hands behind his head and looked very stern.

"Uh, how's that, Daddy?" Claude said, now halfway up to the tractor seat.

"She's outta gas," the old man cackled. "She's outta gas!"

Truck

A five-year association with a van of foreign manufacture ended for us a week ago when the van up and died. It had suffered from time to time with minor ailments but nothing so serious of course as the gut blow that took its life in the parking lot of a supermarket in the next town. Its last words were "Blat-blat!" I had it towed to a car dealer's infirmary, where an autopsy revealed that death came from strangulation; in the vernacular of the mechanic: "She swallered a valve." I hitched home with heavy heart, the bearer of bad news. One among us, I had to tell the family, has passed on.

It seems when death grief busts the insides, *I Remember* is the game the mind in torment plays. My wife said, "Remember the time we took it to California?" "What a time!" I said. "What a time!" "Remember camping along the coast?" she said. "Oh, Greg, remember when somebody broke into it in San Francisco and took your guitar? I thought you were going to cry." "What a time!" I said. I think I said it wistfully. We remembered hundreds of trips with the children sleeping in the back and I remembered in particular one Saturday night in '71, driving across the whole of Tennessee with my family asleep and me listening to the Grand Ol' Opry on the radio and drinking Pabst Blue Ribbon beer and eating cold fried chicken legs.

We went to the front porch to be sorry and to wait for the school bus to bring home our young. These tears of ours were crocodile tears of a fashion because we could, if we wanted, restore life. And that was what we had to discuss. "How much?" she said.

"Seven hundred and fifty dollars, they say," I said.

"Whew," she said. She whistled. "We haven't got it."

"I know."

"Do you want to borrow it?"

"No."

"What do we do with it, then?"

"Trade it."

"Who'd want it?"

"Don't know."

The old school bus topped the hill, dust in its wake, children in its belly, Earl at its wheel, and its brakes screamed as it stopped. The boy got off first and ran toward the house and lost his baseball cap in the process and had to stop and go back and pick it up. He does not like to walk too close to his sister, else people will figure she is his sister; or, at least, that's the way I reckon it. That's the way I was when I was his age. The little girl got off and paused to tidy the Band-Aids on both her knees before checking the mailbox and walking, slowly, humming, kicking rocks, toward the porch. She is a happy child and I envy her contentment and for the life of me cannot figure how she maintains it day in and day out.

The boy came straight out with his problem. "Dad," he said, even before he reached the porch, "there's a girl in my class who keeps on calling me Toad. I've told her and told her and told her I don't like it but she keeps on calling me Toad just the same. I'm gonna knock her brains out!"

"Todd," the boy's mother said. "Don't talk like that."

"Well, I am," he said. I sensed he was resolute, that he had reached the breaking point in this Toad affair, feeling it to be an immeasurable offense on a third grader. His sister came up on the porch and stayed just long enough to scatter the pictures she had colored of birds, fishes and sons of men across our laps, announce her appetite for ice cream and be given the go-ahead. The boy leaned against a porch post and sighed. A world class sigh. "I'll probably break my knuckles when I hit her," he said. He has about him an air of drama that takes over in time of crisis.

"All you've got to do," I said, "is ignore her."

"I've tried," he said. "Tomorrow, old Sue Nell's gonna get it in the face." With that, he went in for ice cream. I followed and told them both, at the kitchen table, that our beloved van was no more.

"Good," the boy said. "Maybe now we can get a truck."

"No," the girl said. "Let's get a Jeep."

Occasionally, not very often but occasionally, children to me seem totally bereft of heart.

Once again by thumb to the next town. On the used car lot in front of the burial ground wherein my van was laid there sat a 1967 half-ton Chevrolet pickup truck, white, the handle Big Bad Bruiser brushed in majestic black script across its cab doors. "Lamar," I said to the white-toothed assistant sales manager ("Call me Lamar," he had said, pumping my hand with both of his.) "I'll swap you my van for that truck."

"Well, Greg," Lamar said, plucking the match from the right side of his mouth and reinserting it on the left, "tell you what we ought do. I'mon go round back and have a close look-see at your van and you be taking a close look-see at the truck meanwhile and when we're done we'll deal. Awright?"

"Awright," I said.

I found that the truck started without difficulty and that the radio worked. I left it idling in neutral, slid out of the cab and opened the hood and stared dumbly at the running six-cylinder engine. That was about the whole of my half of the inspection. By tapping me on the shoulder, Lamar broke the hypnotic state I had entered while watching the fan blades go round for ten or fifteen minutes. "Step round back with me," he said. "There's a few things I need to point out to you 'bout your van—not to downgrade your van, Greg, but just a thing or two I need to point out to you."

We approached my old friend, Lamar's arm around my shoulder.

"You already know, course, I got to put a new engine in her."

I nodded.

"Look at them tires," Lamar said. "Slicker'n owl shit! Whoo-wee! Now, Greg, you know I'd have to put new rubber on the ground before I could front-line her."

I nodded.

"How'd you put that dent in her rear end?"

"I backed into a vicious Pontiac."

"That'll do it," Lamar said. "That'll crease a car awright. Now I don't have to tell you her interior's rough. Real rough. We'd have to do some work in there."

"C'mon, Lamar," I said. "I know everything wrong with it. We don't have to go over it inch by inch."

"Awright, Greg. Tell you what I'mon do. I'mon have to have a hunderd dollars. Gimme a hunderd dollars and drive that truck home today."

"Lamar," I said, "I ain't got a hunderd dollars."

"Let's step inside where it's cool," Lamar said.

Now we were in the air-conditioned office and Lamar had his white-shoed feet on his desk and the rest of him had disappeared into a cloud of cigar smoke. "You know what shape your van's in," Lamar said from within the cloud, "and you know what a clean little pickup that is. And my boss knows them two things too. So give me seventy-five dollars, Greg, and take that little ol' pickup on home."

"Lamar, I ain't got seventy-five dollars."

Lamar fanned the cloud away. "Greg, could you give me a twenty-five-dollar tag fee?"

At dusk, we joy-rode the back roads in Big Bad Bruiser. In celebration we went first to the Dairy Queen and all but stuck our heads in a grease pot. We ordered, it seemed, at least one of everything. I drove that night with a chili dog stain down the front of my shirt. My girl squealed out the window at the fireflies and my wife and I sang along with Waylon Jennings on the radio. My boy was home doing penance for the nosebleed of a classmate.

Home on a Visit

Within days after we moved here, and before we could become patrons, the movie theater in our town closed for lack of business. We missed films, all of us. For a year I kept abreast of what was playing at the drive-in, twenty-five miles to the southwest of us, but nothing ever struck our fancy. In our second summer, out of desperation, we hired a baby-sitter, popped a paper sack full of popcorn, mixed a half gallon of grape Kool-Aid, and drove at sundown to clap eyes on *Hot Summer in Barefoot County*. So bad was it, we were home before the movie had played its length. That night, the baby-sitter paid and gone, the children upstairs asleep (the boy not really asleep, but reading by flashlight to make us think he was asleep), my wife and I talked late, and decided to take a trip to the town where we grew up. Our parents still live there. Holiday would be good for the family, we figured. In the hands of our parents, our children would bloat on sweets, go blind on movies. And we, briefly free from parenthood, would go wild as asylum escapees.

We drove next day to Memphis, Tennessee.

There, our children spent their days in the dark movie houses, their nights on the neon midway of the fairgrounds. My wife played her time in the company of old friends. And I, by curious and coincidental stroke, made the acquaintance of the matinee heroes of my youth. The Third Annual Western Film Festival was in town. I went to look in, and stayed three days.

Right off, I found Lash LaRue, King of the Bullwhip in the old B Westerns. Lash was in the hotel bar, drinking Chivas Regal and milk. Lash was with a drinking companion, a gobby gentleman dressed for Honolulu, who looked like Don Ho gone to seed. I took a seat at the next table, the better to eavesdrop. "God could take your navel and put it right in the middle of your forehead," Lash said to his friend. "He could castrate you and you wouldn't even have the blood changed around. And I myself, Lash LaRue, I could screw your wife from across the room and never even move from this spot!"

"Goddamighty," Lash's buddy screamed, choking on beer. "Haauuch, Thooooeee!" Lash went "Har-har-har" out the side of his mouth and returned to his milk scotch.

I found this bizarre, and moved without drinking to another section of the Hotel Peabody. All fifteen chapters of the 1939 serial *The Lone Ranger Rides Again*, were being shown in the Louis the XVI Room. Bob Livingston played the Lone Ranger. A man named Thundercloud played Tonto. This happened to be a Spanish print. The *William Tell Overture* came on loud and an actor hollered, "It's the Lone Ranger!" But it came out, "—El Lionero Soldierdad!"

At that point, the Louis the XVI Room went black. "What happened?" a voice yelled. "I tripped on the projector cord," a female voice answered meekly. Forty cigarette lighters lit. A small man, down on all fours, cigarette lighter illuminating a rat face, said with discovering glee, "Here the little sumbitch is!" He plugged the cord in the receptacle and the serial resumed. I left quietly, feeling entirely out of synch with my surroundings, thinking I'd better get the lay of this event before plunging into anymore Los Bizarros.

I walked to the Venetian Room, where memorabilia was on sale. And there I ran into an old friend, Tom Fox, the book editor

of the local morning newspaper. He had been poring over the old
posters and studio stills. He had passed over the Roy Rogers, Rex
Allen, and Gene Autry comic books for a sentimental favorite.
"Many a lad first whipped off with a Wonder Woman comic
book," he said, holding up the inspiration.

Across the room, which was enormous, chandeliered, and had
been home to many a Rotarian convention, Fox and I noticed,
and became intrigued with, what appeared to be a Cuban in a
Lone Ranger suit. We investigated. The Lone Ranger turned out
to be Anthony Esposito, a fifth-grade schoolteacher from North-
ford, Connecticut, an old Western buff, a Lone Ranger nut.
"Only three of us in the country have the first thirteen chapters of
the first Lone Ranger serial," he said. "That's the one with Lee
Powell and Chief Thundercloud, whose real name was Victor
Daniels."

I said, "I see by your outfit that you are a cowboy."

"Got the hat and shirt from Bizarre Costumes in New Haven,"
he said. "The guns are exact replicas, only they don't fire. They're
supposed to be .44s. Had to go over the old stills with a magnify-
ing glass to make sure I could get every detail matched, even the
tooling on the holster."

"But boots," I said. "Mr. Esposito, wouldn't you say your side-
zipper ankle highs are a step out of character?"

"The place I went," Mr. Esposito said, "they quoted me a price
of $125 on boots. As it stands now, I'm in better than $300." The
large brown Latin eyes, peering out through slits in the black
mask, took on a moist, frustrated squint. Then the Hispanic Lone
Ranger moaned, "You got to stop somewhere, you know?"

My friend Fox and I wandered away to the information booth,
and found we had just enough time to catch a picture starring
Sunset Carson, another star I admired as a boy. This picture was
Sunset Carson Rides Again. Here is the acting style of Sunset Carson: "If I find the man/ that shot my brother/ I will not need a

gun/ I will kill him/ with my bare hands." And: "I was just think-
ing/ Dan/ how quickly a man's life can change [pause]/ An hour
ago/ I rode into Trail's End without a care in the world/ Now I
have a murder charge over my head." Poetry.

After the movie, Fox said, "Did you know Sunset is in the charity ward over at John Gaston Hospital? He got hit by a car." We
decided to visit the old star.

In the main entrance to John Gaston Hospital, I heard a man
say, "I read in the papers that Sunset Carson is here at the hospital. You know, that Western star? Now, I ask you, what kind of
mother would name a boy Sunset?"

There were sixteen beds in the charity ward where six-foot, six-
inch Sunset Carson lay stretched. All the beds were filled and all
the patients, including Sunset, were in some form of traction.
Legs and arms were suspended, pointing all directions. It was a
pitiful place and Sunset was a pitiful figure, busted up bad with
one small bouquet of zinnias at his side. I said, "How are you,
Sunset?"

"In pain."

I learned, with probing questions, that Sunset was walking
across Elvis Presley Boulevard when a car hit him and sent him
flying thirty-five feet, where he landed gracelessly against the
south wall of Larkin Bearings, Inc. "I was just on my way to get a
hamburger and a milk shake when this car come outta nowhere,"
Sunset explained. "It's got a rear end jacked up about nine foot
and it's full of niggers. So they hit me and they never even stop."

"What do you do for a living now?" I asked.

"Television show in Hickory, North Carolina. I show Westerns
and do commercials."

"Folks from the festival been by to see you?"

"One or two."

"Can I do anything for you?"

"Get me outta here."

"What kind of mother would name a child Sunset?"

"Republic Studios give me that. Real name is Michael Harrison."

On the second day of the festival I met Mitchell Schaperkotter, a huge man, a seventeen-year veteran with the Post Office, the man in charge of the film festival. Schaperkotter said he had been collecting old films since he was a boy. He said his mania led him to buy a theater, the Bristol Theater, the theater of my own boyhood. It was a terribly dirty place. We used to joke that they issued you two sticks with the admission price; one to beat off rats and one to prop up your seat. The floor was sticky and the concession stand was grimy and the screen was cracked and ripped. But we saw all the Westerns there and we went week after week for years and years. Then we learned there was a drive-in across the Mississippi River that was showing nudie movies. And we abandoned the Bristol Theater and its Westerns in favor of tits. And we never turned back.

Mitchell Schaperkotter has owned the Bristol Theater nine years now and he still shows movies starring Gene Autry, who has not made a movie in twenty years. Few children spend weekends at the Bristol. The bulk of customers have not been children for more than twenty-five years.

On the second evening, I met Lash LaRue and learned his life. He is from Gretna, Louisiana, and he never was much of a hand with a gun, a horse or a whip. He was graduated from College of the Pacific in California and he went into real estate with an awful handicap. He had a speech impediment: tongue-tied. But he got his tongue operated on and, being able to speak, even though he did and still does speak directly out the left side of his mouth, he landed some bit parts in the movies. In 1945, they were looking for a guy who could handle a bullwhip for a film called *Song of Old Wyoming*. Alfred LaRue told the director he had been messing with a bullwhip all his life. He won the part as the

Cheyenne Kid. He knew nothing of whips. "I beat myself to death practicing," he told me. He dressed in black, and he got a lot of fan mail. He made about thirty films as Lash LaRue and then he got on the Wyatt Earp television series with Hugh O'Brien and then he found obscurity. And then he found the Lord.

"It happened in 1963," Lash said. "I was watching a restaurant in Reno for a friend of mine. He was having trouble with the cash register and I was watching it for him. They had a full gospel business meeting there one day and the speaker was an ex-bank president from Chicago. A very hip guy. He told about making a sincere commitment to God. I wasn't even involved in the meeting. I was just watching the cash register and kind of half listening.

"He asked if anyone would like to tighten their commitment, to speak up. Nobody said anything and he started to close with a prayer and something happened to me. I felt it. I yelled, 'Hell, man, wait a minute!' My wife thought I had flipped. Anyway, that's the way it happened. My wife left me."

Lash, my hero, sitting there with me in the bar, the Mallard Pub, in a black Naugahyde booth, wearing a black sport coat, black shirt, white string tie, black trousers with a big, white "LL" monogrammed on the right front calf, and black patent leather shoes, turned to me and said, "I would say that I am a triple schizo. That's it. A triple schizo."

"Lash," I said, "are you saying, honest to God, that there are six of you?"

"I myself have had myself checked out. I went to two psychiatrists. One of 'em said, 'I don't understand at all, Lash, but well, uh, good luck to you ol' buddy!'"

There came a page from the lobby. "Telephone for Mr. LaRue. Telephone for Mr. Lash LaRue." Wilma, the bartender, laughed and hollered, "Lash LaRue? Why, that sounds like some kind of fag spade!" Lash ignored the comment, paid his tab, and left for the lobby. In the harsh light of the lobby, his face was the color of bleu cheese, with hairs in it. It was the last time I ever saw him.

On the last day of the festival, I talked with a slip of a man named Johnny Bond, who wrote a dozen songs for Gene Autry and who appeared with Autry on film and on tour. He said he is writing a book called *Gene Autry, Champion.*

"A bunch of us had finished a show one night and we decided we'd go out on the town," Bond recalled. "Gene never would go out. You know, he'd draw a crowd and all. But for some reason this one night he went with us. Well, we were all out on the side-walk outside the hotel about midnight, the streets deserted and all, I forget where we were, and this kind of wino steps out from an alley. Steps right up to Gene and says, 'Well, look what we got here. If it ain't the great white cowboy. Let me tell you some-thing, buddy,' he says. 'You can't sing, you can't act, and you can't ride a horse.'

"Gene stepped up to him real close and he said, 'Friend, you're right. I can't sing. I can't act. I really can't ride a horse. And I've got twenty-five million dollars to prove it.'" We laughed, and Bond asked whether I planned to attend the awards banquet later in the evening. I said I really did not know, that I had been hang-ing around a long time, it seemed.

The grand banquet was in progress on the roof in the Skyway Room of the Peabody Hotel, a place of grandeur and history, the northern tip of the Mississippi Delta, land of Faulkner. I stayed for a long time in the lobby, at the fountain, the fountain fash-ioned from a block of Roman travertine marble, specially quar-ried and imported for the purpose when the Peabody was built in 1925. Ducks swim in the fountain during the day. In late after-noon, a recording of trumpets is played and a bellboy leads the ducks from the fountain, down a red carpet to the elevator, where they ascend to their cage in the penthouse.

This is duck-hunting country. Gentlemen planters used to love the Peabody. Saturday mornings were spent in blinds, on the flat Arkansas side of the wide Mississippi, between the river and the levee. Bourbon was—and is, I'm sure—sipped from Dixie cups. And Saturday nights they would take their ladies to the Skyway Room for big band dancing. The evenings began in rustically elegant dens in the delta. Huge, brown, soft-as-butter leather chairs. Game trophies on the walls. Bourbon from thick-bottomed, field and stream glasses.

Then to the Peabody and into a lobby lined with sixteen huge, square columns, fashioned from Rose St. Genevieve marble, arranged in a rectangle, providing support for a mezzanine balcony from which one could view the elegance of the scene below. The lobby floor strewn elaborately with thick rugs. Six hundred and twenty-five rooms in the stories above.

All that is no more, just as the actors above me in the once grand Skyway Room are no longer famous. Each was being presented a plaque. "All I can say is thank you from the bottom of my heart." "I'm grateful and privileged. Thank you." "Thank you. Thank you. Thank you."

We stayed around the city for another week, and I thought with each day less and less about all the old heroes. It had been pathetic, and I had, out of some morbid curiosity, continued to look on.

A few weeks after we were home, we heard the Peabody Hotel had gone bankrupt and was shut down. And in a town fifty miles from us, Lash LaRue had been arrested and charged with possession of marijuana. Lash was telling the authorities that he had picked up two hitchhikers and, upon discovering they carried marijuana, he had swapped them his Bible for the dope. He had intended to save them, he said. Unfortunately, he failed to ditch the grass.

In Memphis, Lash had said, "I'm doing all right now. I got me a red Eldorado Cadillac."

He had been asked, "Where do you sleep, Lash?"

"In the back of the Cadillac."

My Friend Eural

I was down to the pool hall earlier today, having a word with Eural, who is by consensus the meanest man in the state. It was Eural who, the night before his brother was to stand trial for some small felony, set fire to the courthouse. Eural's logic, eminent by our hill standards: "Can't hold no trial if they don't have no courthouse."

The bar of justice, temporarily situated in a mobile home on the square where the courthouse once stood, saw fit to free Eural's brother, and, later in the year, to free Eural himself, who had suffered official accusal of arson. At the time, Eural observed caustically, "You don't beat nothin' when you got to pay ten thousand dollars for a thinkin' lawyer."

Eural and I had what is called a wide-ranging conversation, touching on all the high-minded topics: Kissinger; the law; the high price of sugar, which brought death to moonshining; safety regulations on dirt track racing, which brought death to dirt track racing; airplanes; citizens band radios; and the Williams' Base Hit pinball machine, on which I had just won Eural's admiration.

I suppose, if I had not racked up twenty free games, lighting every light, ringing every bell, causing quite a commotion in my corner of the concrete block building, painted green, I never would have gotten Eural's attention. A boy, nine I judged him, stayed by my elbow throughout the winning, his face showing reverence if ever I saw it. Tiring of the pinball (I *teethed* on a Williams' Base Hit), I turned over the free games to my statistician. Stepping by the pool table, its green felt worn white in patches, I heard, "You pretty damn good on that machine." It was Eural, who had for the third time swept the house in Eight Ball. Fate connected us: two Saturday heroes.

Of course, I had heard of Eural. Once, on a Sunday drive with some friends who have lived here longer than we, I passed his house, which is hard to see from the road, sitting as it does behind a thousand automobile carcasses. And to the east of the dead car lot was, I recall, a dug-out area big as a strip mine, and on its far rim, a houseboat sitting on sawed-off utility poles, the houseboat giving the hole in the red clay the look of a dried-up lake. "God," I said. "What happened over there?" "That used to be a speedway," one of my friends said. "Ol' Eural Mabry the meanest man in the state used to run it." It is always said that way, as if Eural's surname were "state," not Mabry. "That's his house over behind the junk lot." Since the day of that drive, I've heard tales of the legendary Eural, and, twice or more, his person has been pointed out to me in town. "That's him." Always in hushed tones, as if Eural might actually overhear—and dismember us.

And so at the pool hall it was with great horror I accepted Eural's introduction and handshake.

"Eural Mabry."

"Greg Jaynes."

"What you do—other'n pinball?"

"Write."

"Write?"

"Yes."

"Knew one once't."

"One what?"

"Writer."

"Chase't him all over White County. Just wanted to talk to him 'bout a little ol' thing." Eural laughed, showing solid, square white teeth. His companions, who had begun another game at the pool table, straightened their backs and laughed with Eural. Eural put a grease-grimed hand, size and weight of a motorcycle battery, on my shoulder, and kneaded it. At this moment I thought, "Don't hit me."

Turned out, the local Union 76 (I believe it to be the former Phillips 66) had been burglarized and its owner, a poor man, did not have insurance enough to cover the loss. The thief took everything, fan belts and all, pirated tapes of rock-and-roll stars, everything, and the sheriff, feeling sorry for the victim, came to Eural, who is, after all, the meanest man in the state and would be expected to know who took what and why—and where it went, and who has it now?—and said, "Eural, help me get ol' Jimmy's merchandise back, would you now?" So Eural made one telephone call, to be exact, and found out where everything was, and took his truck and went and got it. Eural's thanks: a story in the newspaper saying, in essence, the sheriff had a thief solve the case. "And when I seen that writer over'n White County, I was just gonna pinch his head off, that's all," Eural told me, and we laughed, and he let go my shoulder.

Now Eural was sucking on a Yoo-Hoo, the chocolate drink from Yogi Berra, and I had my Fanta grape and the two of us leaned against the hood of a Jeep parked outside the pool hall on this, a gray-skied Saturday in September in the year preceding the United States of America's Bicentennial, a year in which everything would turn red, white and blue, including toilet seats; a year that would frustrate Eural, because he wouldn't be able to get a piece of that action, because he couldn't work any patriotic angle on his business, which is smashing dead cars into flat strips of iron, and selling the iron for scrap. "Ever time I turn on the TV they're talkin' 'bout that Bicentennial slop," Eural said. He drained his bottle and wiped his mouth on the back of his hand and he said disgustedly, "Hell-fire!"

It began to rain.

I said, "How come you closed your race track?"

"State."

"State?"

"Too much interference from the state. They was gonna force me to buy sixty thousand dollars' worth of new lights. And the insurance went up sky high. They made me keep a ambulance at the track all the time. So I got me this ol' hearse, believe it was a '46 Cadillac, and I painted MEAT WAGON 'long the sides. Ever time some driver got the wind knocked outta him, I'd thow him in the back and head out. Shocks was so bad on that ol' hearse, time I got to the highway, ol' boy I was haulin' would be all right."

"Ever have a bad accident at your track?"

"Worse thing ever happened was Cecil Stephenson run a screwdriver through his hand."

I moved out of the rain, under the overhang from the pool hall roof. Eural stood in the rain. Eural, a brick house of a man in overalls, hair black, eyes gray like a two-lane blacktop a decade in the sun, used his index fingers like windshield wipers to clear the water from his eyebrows and said, "Reckon we oughta move in the Jeep?" We sat in the Jeep, sheltered by a cloth top.

"I took up airplanes," Eural said. "You ever hear of C. W. Houston?"

I said no.

"Best pilot in this part of the country. Best pilot this side of the Mississippi, I'd say. I'm the one what saved his life one time, sort of."

"How's that?"

"Well," Eural said, bringing his booted foot up to rest on the walnut gearshift knob, "C.W. was out cuttin' the fool."

"Cuttin' the fool?"

"Cuttin' the fool. In a Piper Cub. Swappin' ends. And flyin' upside down. All them fancy things. Just one thing he did wrong: he cut it a little too close over a pasture down at the south end of Forsyth County. Wing on that Piper Cub come up under two strands of barbed wire. I don't even think ol' C.W. felt it at first. Plane just kept on a-goin', pullin' that barbed wire along, poppin' them fence posts out, but when he come to that corner post, where the barbed wire's wrapped around three-four times, brought that airplane up short, I'll tell you that. Flipped her over in a briar patch."

"Hurt C.W.?"

"Well, I'm gettin' to that," Eural said. "I'm gettin' to that. Ol' C.W. commenced hollerin', 'Mayday! Help! Help! Mayday! Mayday!' I was out in my truck and I heard him on my CB radio. I got him to calm down a minute and tell me where he was at, so I drove on over there.

"One thing you got to understand about your Piper Cub. She's a good little airplane, but she's got a little ol' crossbar underneath the dashboard, or control panel, or whatever you want to call it. Well, ol' C.W., when he hit the ground, somehow he got pinned under there, had his leg caught tighter'n a vise. So I park my truck and I come runnin' up on him and he's yellin', 'Eural, get me outta here! For God's sake, get me outta here!' Now your engine's right up front there on the nose of that airplane. And she was hot. I'm standin' there, and I'm hearin' that gasoline fryin' on that engine, and I know she's gonna blow any minute, and ol' C.W.'s just a-hollerin'.

"I tell you I just don't know what to do."

"What'd you do?"

"I'm gettin' to that. So I'm hearin' this gasoline just a-fryin', and I ain't got a thing with me to cut C.W. loose, and he's just a-hollerin' so much I can't think straight, so I wrap my arms under his, grab him round the chest, and I yank. I give it all I got. And all the time I'm pullin' on him, C.W.'s screamin', 'Don't hurt me, Eural!' and makin' a awful racket. But I got him out. I got him outta there, all right. Broke his leg in three places—here, here, and here."

"Phew!" I said to Eural, wiping my brow, deeply relieved. "That was a hell of a story."

"Yep," Eural said. "Course ol' C.W. won't even speak to me no more. I can see him on the street and he won't even thow up his hand to me."

"How's that?" I said. "Because you broke his leg?"

"Well, that's part of it," Eural said. "For one thing, that airplane didn't catch fire. And for another, ol' C.W. walks with a kind of a limp now."

Eural told me Henry Kissinger was going to drag us all to hell in a bucket.

Eural told me how, with the use of a citizens band radio, we could successfully burglarize the house of the richest man in our area, the man who sells propane gas to all of us. I will not go into this, because it involves certain missing properties in the minds of our region's finest investigators.

When it stopped raining, and I got out of the Jeep, Eural told me that he would see me around. "See you around," he said. "Sure thing," I said, suspecting I had struck up an association you don't run bragging about.

Once More to the Deer

At my friend's direction, I turned left into the gravel drive, drove past an enormous fig tree, and stopped back of the woodshed. I could see by the light of the full white moon the house and all the outbuildings. They sat in symmetrical arrangement on the lip of a one-hundred-twenty-acre farm. The house, huge, with unpainted pine weatherboarding, sitting hard by the asphalt road, supported by piers of varying material—here brick, there cinder block. Preconstructed, concrete steps were affixed to the side porch. Beyond the house was the woodshed, with stove wood piled the height of the average man. To the right of the woodshed was a tool shed, containing all manner of farm implements. And farther back, standing black and high pitched in the moonlight, was a barn the size of a warehouse. Disturbed by our entrance, two white-faced heifers stuck their noses through the gate to the left of the barn and groaned low their annoyance. "This is it," my friend said. "Want to stretch a little before going in?" The grass was wet.

We had been driving a long time. Huey, a friend, and O'Briant, a friend whose birthplace we had now reached, told funny, self-effacing stories the whole way. Both of them ate from a pound bag of M & Ms chocolate-covered peanuts as I drove, and O'Briant, who sat by the window, was charged with keeping in receiving shape the straightened clothes hanger I was using for a radio antenna. In the back we carried the stock of the hunter: shotguns and ammunition, fleece-lined coats, thermal underwear, woolen socks, boots, sour mash whisky. It had been cold, with cold air coming through the wing flaps that will not close, and our noses became faucets while our feet sweated from the heat produced by the heater in the truck cab. The November moon afforded us sharp silhouettes of textile mills long before we neared them and our headlights showed clear the ugly brick buildings squatting next to rivers that ran slow. We had gone through dark mill town after dark mill town on this late night ride to a South Carolina farm and finally, about two in the morning, I was told, "Turn left. We're here."

Two small dogs of uncertain breed surrounded us, yapping, gradually tightening their circle, Indian style. We made our way toward the barn, bore right, and came to a stop just shy of a scuppernong arbor. We stood there limbering, stamping our feet on the wet ground. I could smell, but could not see, the pigpen. Providentially, the whisky bottle appeared in Huey's hand.

I asked, "Where's the privy?" "Just over there in the shadows," O'Briant said. "You'll find it when the time comes." The bottle circled. O'Briant told of being a boy, getting ready for school, arranging his books and notebooks in a tidy pile on the front steps and, being dressed and fed, going back inside to watch television. When he heard the school bus, he ran out, grabbed his books and boarded. He did not know until after he had taken a seat that, in his absence, a yard dog had taken unerring aim and soaked down his schoolbooks. His classmates quickly picked up the scent. It was a stigma he carried with him throughout his days in the elementary grades.

We all told of being a boy, and the embarrassing incidents that accompany that time of life. The bottle circled, circled again. We were warm now. "What's in the barn?" I said. "Everything," O'Briant said. "This is great," Huey said. "How come," I said, "if you had a television, and conveniences like that, you still don't have indoor plumbing here?" "My grandfather lived with us until he died last year," O'Briant said. "He looked on it as some sort of invasion. Everybody went along with him. That's why I went out for sports in high school. I could always take a shower before I came home. A nice hot shower." The bottle reached my hand. Hand to mouth. Swallow. Grimace. Smile a wicked smile. Back of other hand wipes mouth. Reflexes perfect. Our behavior, it comes to me, is the behavior of seniors on prom night.

"You think we'll get a deer?" Huey asks.

"Don't know," O'Briant says. "There's plenty of 'em here. My father plants peas for 'em."

"You ever kill a deer?" Huey asks.

"No," O'Briant says. "You?"

"No," Huey says. "You?"

"No," I say. "And I'm not sure I want to."

"What kind of tree is that?"

"Pecan."

"Doesn't look like a pecan tree."

"Well, it is."

"What time are we going hunting?"

"About five."

"What time is it now?"

"About three-thirty."

"Jesus!"

"Whew!"

"Are we ever gonna feel bad!"

"Better go in."

"Yeah."

"Yeah."

Huey sticks the bottle under his shirt. O'Briant lets us in through the kitchen door. The house is cold. We step carefully round a long kitchen table, then through another door and into a great hall. I have seen this construction before. The hall runs the length of the house, with rooms off to either side. In this house there are six big rooms, the great hall, a front, side and back porch. No drinking is allowed in the house.

O'Briant shows us the room we will share. He plans to sleep in the hall, in a bed outfitted with an electric blanket. We shut the bedroom door, promising to go directly to bed, to make no noise, to be, in short, good boys. The bottle reappears. The iron bed tiptoes from one side of the room to the other. The hundred-watt bulb hanging by cord from the twelve-foot ceiling commences a slow, concentric swirl. Of its own accord, like the bed and the bulb, the unlit gas heater fires on. A chamber pot skips across the linoleum floor, losing its hat in the process, noiselessly kisses the wallboard, and returns to its original roost. The very chair on which I sit falls over. The bare bulb goes dark and a flashlight pattern appears on the ceiling. I hear a fool giggle.

A hand on my shoulder, kneading it. A voice in my ear: "Get up. Breakfast."

Huey and I should not have been allowed to clothe ourselves for the same reason spastics are not allowed to be air traffic controllers. A wall knocks us to the floor. On purpose, a dresser sticks its foot out and trips us.

Breakfast has no flavor. I perceive, but do not see, an old woman tending to us. I perceive, but do not feel the heat from, a wood stove. I place elbows on the table, palms to temples, and slowly, painfully, open my eyes and slowly, with tremendous effort, begin to focus. The plate is dun colored. There are scrambled eggs there beside sausage patties, and at two o'clock there stands a mound of grits topped by a pat of butter, a vivid yellow eye staring up at me. Slowly, I lift my head, extending my vision and focus by inches: now reaching the pepper shaker, now to the orange juice, now approaching another dun plate, above the plate a wretched, rheumy-eyed, alabaster white-faced wraith I once knew as Huey, and beyond Huey, in a dark corner, a man, by God I swear! a man posing as a tree.

"This is Ronnie." It is O'Briant's voice, but I cannot find his body. The tree stands and smiles and says hello, then sits again. "We'll get 'em today," the tree says. Despite the inconstant pounding behind my left eye, I force myself to give Ronnie a hard look. He is wearing overalls bearing a pattern the shape and color

of leaves. His face is painted green and black. His neck is painted green and black. I can see by the tops that he wears a perfectly good pair of combat boots, but he has chosen to cover them with black socks. Ronnie, I am told, will be our guide.

The next thing I remember is climbing up a ladder and finding, somewhere around elevation ten or twelve feet, a plywood seat attached to a persimmon tree. I mounted the seat, swung my legs around the tree and embraced the tree with my arms. "You're not gonna hunt that way, are you?" I look down to find it is the voice of the man with the painted face. He is holding my borrowed Winchester 243 and my borrowed box of Remington cartridges. I turn around so that my back is to the tree and he hands me up my arsenal. Then he and my friends disappear into the woods.

It is still dark and I am shivering. My rifle is laid across my lap. I calculate that I have had twenty minutes of sleep and I have never behaved more stupidly. I begin to nod, to fight it, to nod, to fight it. Overhead, blackbirds caw at one another. Below, a squirrel sashays by, convinced, no doubt, he is in no danger. For that matter, neither is the next squirrel, nor the next, nor the rabbit that follows them. The sun rises and I still have not loaded my rifle.

Hours later, we walked down a dirt road that led to an abandoned house where O'Briant's mother was born. Along the road, we saw the fresh tracks of a half-dozen deer, two rabbits and a dog. In conference, we also found that we could not have killed a deer even if one had met our sights. Huey had brought along twelve-gauge ammunition for a sixteen-gauge shotgun. O'Briant had an M-1 carbine with a faulty firing pin. I refused to load. The tree had some primitive firearm that last saw action with the Rough Riders.

But, feeling better, we rejoiced in the beauty of the day. A clear, cold sky, with a slight breeze moving the milkweed that grew around the abandoned house, and moving too the long pods on the locust trees, and the ornamental plum, and the mulberry. Wasps swarmed in and out the paneless windows, and the tin roof, long gone to rust, matched the color of the maple leaves.

None of us even felt piqued when Ronnie, the consummate hunter, even to the point of wearing socks on his boots to quiet his step, told us he had taken three bucks so far this season. We went to town for a chocolate milk shake to settle our stomachs and returned to the house as the women were laying out lunch for the mob.

The old woman who is serving has taken her chair by the cupboard. We are eating. "Ronnie come back one day and say he got two, no three buck. Say he got 'em all in one morning. Larry go over to help him bring 'em back and, turns out, what he killed first time was a limb. Other one was a little ol' thang weigh mebbe fifty pound. Couldn't find the other one." She laughed.

On the table were biscuits, cornbread, butter beans, cheese and macaroni, pork chop pie, ham, slaw, pork roast, sweet potato pie and lemon poundcake. Around the table were men—the head of the house, O'Briant's father, an uncle, a brother, O'Briant, Huey, me, and, later on, Ronnie, who had washed the paint from his face. Ronnie wore a weedy beard. "Look just like a monkey, don't he?" the old woman cackled. We came to find that Ronnie was the suitor of a sister who lived in the house. By family consensus, he was a better suitor than last year's, a young man who thought he bore a striking resemblance to Burt Reynolds and who went around asking, "Don't you think I look like Burt Reynolds?"

Each time iced tea in my glass fell below rim level, the old woman refilled the glass. In this house, the women serve. They do not eat with the men, I came to find. When the men are done, they clean after them, then sit down to have their meal and to gossip, and when they are through, they make preparations for the meal to follow. It has always been this way. In the course of meals, I committed several errors. I tried several times to say "thank you" to the women. This is not done. Worse, once I tried to take my plate, glass and silverware to the wash pan. This simply is not done. More on the women: Huey and I found the bedroom we had sacked had been restored and disinfected while we were away in the morning. O'Briant, a child of the house, returned to find his dirty clothes had been laundered and pressed, even his underwear had been pressed, and stacked in a neat pile on his pillow. I don't know to this day how many women live in that house. It seemed we were served by a different woman at each meal.

Foundered by the meal, we sat taking the sun on the front porch. The elder O'Briant, a short, stout, quiet man with a week's growth of white whiskers on his face, joined us for a while. "See any tracks?" he asked.

"Some."

"Can't even make stew out of tracks," he said.

"Do you hunt? Or fish?" I asked.

"Nope. Don't have the patience for fishing. Don't have the time for hunting."

I moved out to the yard to sleep for a while beneath a chinaberry tree. The last thing I saw was the sun glinting off the yellow balls of fruit.

In the late afternoon we hunted again, again unsuccessfully. O'Briant killed a beer can with a .22 single shot rifle. We ate a jar of Penrose sausages.

That night, after another meal that brings out the gluttony in a man, we drove twenty-five miles to the nearest town of any size and O'Briant visited the hamburger haven of his youth. He ordered and consumed a steak sandwich and a baked potato. It made me sick to watch him do it. We slept as tuckered, full fellows will. Huey and I made no racket.

In the morning there were cheese biscuits and grits and bacon and coffee. We walked the woods feeling fine, the pine straw wet underfoot, a martin pestering a hawk overhead, a bobwhite whistling in the bush. Coming upon the abandoned old house, I decided to situate myself at a window in the loft. The stand would give me a clear view of the road where we had seen tracks the day before. O'Briant and Huey went off down to the swamp.

About an hour after sunup, I saw movement in the shadows a

hundred yards or so down the road. I was still undecided about shooting anything. I made sure the safety was on, threw the rifle to my shoulder, and sighted down the scope, a maneuver to bring within focus whatever I had seen. I saw myself as using the rifle much as a peaceful man would use a pair of binoculars. The cross hairs in the scope came to rest on the forehead of O'Briant's father. I put the gun down and hunted no more.

A fried chicken lunch. Guitar playing and singing beneath a catalpa tree. A long drive home.

"That's a beautiful place," I told O'Briant.

"Not to spend your whole life," he said. I dropped him at his new brick home in the city, a place with two bathrooms.

The Deep Winter Black Dog Blues

All day, all night, all day the next day, all week rain sets in here in the winter. It beats down our spirits and dulls our brains and somewhere in late January, long before the rains let up, we find ourselves uncomfortable in one another's company. I shout at the children without provocation. My wife stops speaking at all. She glowers, sulks, reads. This is a small house, and it becomes entirely too close when the winter holes us up. The constant noise of rain hitting the tin roof is torture, not romance, but audio punishment. All the bright plans made in the clear fall days turn amorphous. I do not know what I am about. I lose track; we, all of us, do. I worry. I slog through the mud to the barn and throw the hay and the feed at the pony. I slog through the mud back to the house, ducking beneath the wet clothes that have been on the line for days. I slam the door, walk past the washing machine filled with sopping clothes, the same sopping clothes that have been there for days, and I sit at the kitchen table and all but dare anyone to speak. I do not exaggerate the drama. At this writing, we are three weeks into the rain siege and three weeks into our second winter here.

What is the cause? The mountains, perhaps. Once the clouds get to this valley, they are caught. They hang low. I can't see the mountain across the road because the clouds block it out. And the road ruts and ruts more and the road tears hell out of the shocks on the truck and the car and the steering becomes so loose that you can turn the wheel half a turn and still get no response. Nothing works right in winter. We get leaks in the roof. I cannot find a day dry enough to crawl up and pour the slimy pitch that is supposed to plug the roof holes and does, for a while, but never for long.

This bad case of the winter black dog blues makes me wonder what we are doing here. In the fall, the summer and the spring I know. In the winter I think about money. If I had money we would winter someplace else. Why don't I have money? Because I don't work. Why don't I work? Because I'm unemployable, marked for rest, something. Why don't I farm then, commercially, I mean, be a flat-out honest to God farmer? Because this is no time to go into farming. I'd lose my shirt. I have no shirt to lose. Yes, I do. It's hanging outside on the line—in the rain.

The rain has washed the topsoil from the slope back of the house. Before we moved here, a former owner (a fool, as it turned out) brought in a dozer and scraped the slope and set up a trailer. The trailer is long gone. The damage remains. I sowed rye and fescue back there last spring, to stop the erosion, but we didn't get enough rain (my God!) at the crucial time, and not enough grass came up.

Setting my rant to paper does not exorcise the depression, so I will quit it—right after one more lowdown note:

In the city the other night, for express purposes of wassail, I met a man I had not seen in seven years. He asked, "What are you up to now?"

"I live on a farm north of here."

"Oh," he said, and his face brightened from curiosity. "Are you farming?"

"No," I said. "Hiding."

Lamar Fountain Is Free

I see by the news that Lamar Fountain, my fellow shut-in, has been paroled. High time! Mr. Fountain was imprisoned, unjustly, I hasten to say, many years ago. He himself made matters worse— aggravated his situation as a boy does a scabby knee—by refusing to serve out his sentence. Time and time again, Mr. Fountain ran lickety-split from our state's penal institutions. I have maintained close monitor on his struggle.

Believe it was a year ago this month when I read an account of Mr. Fountain's seventh, make that eighth, escape, and found myself in the following week driving through his county on my way elsewhere. The word was he had never been caught. The law said his pattern was to stay gone about six weeks, drink bottle upon bottle of whisky, then come dragging himself back to jail, frazzle worn as a bent-dicked dog. I am a sucker for this manner of behavior; it interests me far more than, say, Sunday football on television.

The egg-shaped man at the general store in the town Mr. Fountain calls home told me the sheriff's name was Gaskins, Walter Gaskins, and that he could be found down to the courthouse most anytime, day or night. So I went down to the courthouse in the daylight and a deputy let me in the door and showed me into

Sheriff Gaskins' office. Sheriff Gaskins was on the telephone. He made a wipe sweep of his hand and motioned me to sit on a green Naugahyde couch. I noticed the sheriff had a yellow nose, the only man I've ever seen who had such. This is what the sheriff was saying on the telephone:

"Did he do anything other'n pinch you on the titty? Uh-hmmm. I see. Put your hand on his private. I see. Well, hmmmm, uh, how did his private feel to you? No, ma'am. I don't mean good or bad . . ." Directly, the sheriff polished off the delicate complaint. "Well," he said to the caller, "come on down and we'll take out a warrant on the bastard."

In response to his first question, I told the sheriff no, I did not have a complaint. I asked him to tell me about Lamar Fountain. The sheriff is a brusque man. Here is what he said:

"I'm going down there tonight in my old '52 Chevrolet and I'm not gonna take a gun and I'm not gonna take a deputy and I'm gonna come back with Lamar or I ain't. Anybody don't like what I'm doing, they can kiss my ass." Given the alternative, I assured the sheriff of my firm, unshakable support.

Sheriff Gaskins rose, came round front of his desk, leaned back on it, looked at me sternly and told me the only reason Lamar was out of jail again was to spend his inheritance. A tractor turned over on his daddy and killed him, and Lamar stood to get eight hundred dollars and a nice piece of land, so the sheriff said. The sheriff said Lamar's relatives had already fronted him to the eight hundred and that the escapee had been flashing money all over town. "Leland Kent will tell you," the sheriff said. He gave me directions to Leland Kent's grocery store.

"He come in here the other day," Mr. Kent said of Mr. Fountain. "He got some beanie weenies, Vienna sausage, pork 'n' beans, light bread, sardines, some of them little ol' oatmeal cookies, and a quart of buttermilk. He got some Clorox, too. Said he wanted it for his athlete's foot, but I knowed different. I knowed what he wanted it for. Tell me if you put that Clorox on your shoes it'll keep the dogs off your trail.

"So he gets ten, twelve dollars' worth and he laid a hundred-dollar bill on the counter. I said, 'Lamar, I don't believe I can change that.' He said, 'Just jot it down. I'll be back tomorrow.' And he did, too. Musta been fifty officers and two, three high sheriffs around here lookin' for him, and Lamar walked right on into my store and bought some more beanie weenies and such. Course, I been knowin' him ever since he was little bitty . . ."

I asked Mr. Kent where a thirsty man might find a beer, here in swamp country, and, on his recommendation, I drove to the Silver Dollar Restaurant, a roadside establishment that does not sell food. The Silver Dollar sits on sand beneath tall slash pines that look sick. Mr. Fountain may find beauty in it, but I could not. Where the land isn't thick with gallberry bushes and huckleberry bushes and palmettos, it is planted in tobacco, corn and peanuts. There isn't a hill within one hundred miles of that county. Everyone inside the concrete block Silver Dollar was talking about Lamar Fountain.

Jimmy the bartender, a man with no neck to speak of, was saying, "Ol' Lamar is kinda like that, what's that fellow in the movie? Cool Hand Luke. Yeah, that's Ol' Lamar for you," when I pulled a stool up to the black-padded bar. There was red shag carpeting on the wall behind the bar and spaced three feet apart along the carpeting were diamond-shaped mirrors.

"I growed up with Lamar," said Earl, a customer who sat to my left, sucking on a Miller's. "Course he's older'n me. Guess Lamar's about forty-eight now. I bet he's prob'ly up in New York City right this minute havin' himself a drink at some bar."

"And he'll prob'ly come back here," said Jimmy the bartender, "in an Eldorado Cadillac and take the sheriff out to lunch."

"Naw," said Ernest, the janitor, who is six feet nine or better. No egg, Ernest. "Lamar hauled ass. He won't be back."

"Now that's where you're wrong," said a man with red hair and a nail body with tight, knotty muscles all over it. A backhoe driver for the county, I learned later. "This is home to Lamar."

"Tell me," Jimmy the bartender said, wiping clean the counter, and then he dropped the sentence and looked at me. "Beg pardon," he said. "Didn't notice you come in. Somethin' for you?"

"Draft."

"You got it," Jimmy said, drawing one. "Tell me Lamar's been usin' tar cups. Them cups of turpentine they get off the pine trees. Say he heats it up, puts it on the soles of his shoes, lets it cool and then he walks pretty as you please anyplace he wants to in them swamps. No scent."

"Pepper, too," Earl said. "Black pepper'll flat THOW a dog off a track."

"They run him with the dogs four days straight," Jimmy said. "Next day, Lamar showed up out back of his sister's place, washin' the sweat out of his clothes. Tol' the boys down at the store the dogs come within ten foot of him, and he was settin' on a log, eatin' oatmeal cookies and drinkin' buttermilk. Went right by him. Another beer, Earl?"

I had business in a neighboring state, and thus could spend no more than an afternoon in that county far to the south of us. At the Silver Dollar, the talk turned to mules right after Jimmy said, "Sheriff Gaskins took Lamar to prison one day and Lamar come on back home that night." There was time left to visit Sheriff Gaskins one short while more.

> Lamar Fountain was not a bad man;
> He went to prison in this great land.
> Whisky and women were the cause of it all;
> That's been many a man's downfall.
> Poor Lamar Fountain!

The sheriff was singing, accompanying himself on guitar, chording it with one finger. It was his own composition, "The Ballad of Lamar Fountain."

> Many days and nights have come and gone
> Since Lamar left his loved ones at home
> He suffered many days and nights away,
> Thinking of his parents who were old and gray.
> Poor Lamar Fountain.

The sheriff let up and said to me, "Lamar's got a weakness. It's whisky. Now, even me, I like whisky. But sometimes I do somethin' under the influence that you wouldn't do when you were at yourself. That's what landed Lamar in trouble."

> A man with no money can only say
> With God's help he'll be free someday.
> As a law-enforcement officer I can't stand
> To see advantage took of any poor man.
> Poor Lamar Fountain!

The sheriff stood the guitar in a corner and explained that back in 1968 Lamar got drunk with another fellow. The other fellow gave Lamar a twenty-dollar bill and told him to fetch more whisky. "Lamar didn't come back in the proper time," he said. The drinking partner got a warrant, charging Lamar with robbery. He was advised—ill advised, it is thought—to plead guilty and accept a suspended sentence. He did so, and got euchred, sentenced to go to jail. No one said anything about a suspended sentence. "Ever' time he escapes," the sheriff said, "they give him one to five years more. Here lately, I think they've been givin' him five years ever' time."

At the time I was there, Lamar Fountain, six foot three, 180 pounds and a "pretty boy to look at," had been loose over a month. The Law was embarrassed, even though Sheriff Gaskins was more than sympathetic. "Lamar ain't no damned escape artist," the sheriff said. "It's negligence on somebody's part, I can tell you that. You just peck on concrete long enough and you peck a hole in it. You take out the block and you get away. That's all Lamar done. We'll get him."

Night after night, the posse had formed outside Leland Kent's Grocery, where the sign on the door said, "If You Owe Me Please Pay Me As I Need It." Time after time, members of the posse bought soft drinks and cigars and Goody's Headache Powders and prepared for work. Sheriff Gaskins got astride his horse, his Doberman pinscher at his side. A great howling began and the bloodhounds were loosed. There was a mad dash across the two-lane blacktop and the manhunt was in the swamp.

By midnight, two nights before I was there, the dogs had turned up one old swamp rabbit. Wet, tuckered men were heaving for breath. They had followed paths so thickly overgrown, according to the sheriff's account, that they had to travel them on hands and knees. They had found three camps Lamar had used. They gave up for the evening.

Next day, Sheriff Gaskins was out on his horse when he found Lamar Fountain's current hiding place. There was a bed of hay, with a tin roof supported by six pine saplings. Beanie weenie and Vienna sausage cans were piled all around, filled with cigarette butts.

"I heard him hit the woods," the sheriff said. "My dog hadn't run but one man, and I didn't trust him. So I called back for the bloodhounds." All the dogs and the sweating men plunged in after Lamar, who was leading by less than five minutes. They ran him all afternoon. They did not catch him.

Now it has been a year, and Lamar has been caught and freed, legally. They had found him peacefully fishing for bream and crappie in a pond not far from his sister's house. According to the newspapers, he threw up his hands and said he was tired.

A great Free Lamar Fountain wave struck the south of the state. Petitions were signed and delivered. Attorneys went to work in his behalf without pay. And today, success. Lamar is quoted as saying, "I am tickled to death." He said he has stopped drinking, and that he intends to farm and live a quiet, respectable life. I am told that Sheriff Gaskins, and all who know Lamar Fountain, believe he will live a free man the rest of his days.

To Work, She Goes

Late last night, about the time the old Frigidaire started humming in the kitchen and shaking the floorboards all over the house, my wife turned on her pillow and said, "Are you happy here?"

"For the most part," I said. I had thought she was sleeping.

"Do you think it's possible we'll stay here for the rest of our lives?"

"No," I said, and I said it without really thinking about it. I didn't have to. The term "for the rest of our lives" is far beyond my shilly-shally range. It will be years before I can use it with any resolve.

"Why?" I said. "You got problems?"

"Sort of." She put her head in the crook of her elbow. "Are you interested in that?"

I closed the book and put it on the nightstand. "What's wrong?"

"Let's get up. I'd like some coffee." She slid out of bed, pulled on a robe and left the room. She moved quickly and I was given no vote in the matter. I would have favored for staying in a warm bed and talking.

There was coffee when I got to the kitchen. The two cats were asleep against the dog's belly, the three of them curled before the small gas space heater. The Frigidaire had gone quiet. My wife was searching the cupboard for cups with handles. Most of our cups are amputees. "Look here," she said, "I need some sign, some indication, of what we plan to do. You don't ever talk about the future. I mean, what are we going to do? I mean it."

"God," I said, "your voice is strident."

"Strident? I'm concerned. I'm serious. You never talk about the future. Every once in a while you mention building a new house over in the high meadow. That's as far as it goes. That's as far as you go. Do you have one plan in this whole world?"

"Sounds to me like you're thinking about moving."

"I don't want to move—get the cream out, would you?—I want to make plans. I want to talk about me going back to school, or me opening the bookstore on the square, like I've been thinking about, and us building the new house, or totally redoing this one. I can't start a business if you think we're temporary. There's no sense in taking the veterinary courses if I'm going to drop out in the middle of a school year. There's no reason in starting anything if I'm not going to finish it. And you . . ." She was actually glowering at me as she poured the coffee. "You, you're so hazy about, about *everything!*"

I didn't say anything. I shut the refrigerator door and the motor cranked on again, making the floor vibrate. She had me truly pegged. Here lately, about the only interest I take in the future is wishing, now and again, that the scarlet maples I planted out front will grow tall, full and straight in phenomenally short time. Except for occasional bouts with the deep winter rat-suck funk, I am happy here and content to stay. "I'm pretty selfish, I guess," I said, sitting down.

"You are," she said. She didn't sound harsh anymore, though. She even went so far as to relax that pinched, worried expression, but she did not smile. "Look, for the first time in our lives, both the kids are in school. They're in school all day. I'm feeling kind of ineffectual. All these years I've been a mother and I've been your wife and I've done the pottery trip and the macrame trip and all those jillion other things housewives do and now I'm ready to get on with it. I might be a butcher or I might be a para-vet or just, just about anything. But I need to know your plans. You can understand that, can't you?"

"If you went down tomorrow and enrolled in a two-year course, do you actually think I'm so insensitive I'd insist we uproot right in the middle of it?"

"No," she said. "It's not that. I know you'd go along with whatever. It's my choice. I'll make it. But I need to know, for my own peace of mind, how you see our future. Say I open a florist shop. Or a nursery. Will that hurt us? Will that turn out to be a conflict?"

I said, "Once you make up your mind, then we'll have to set about getting something harmonious arranged. I'm very flexible. Try me." I got up to reheat the coffee.

"What will you be doing in five years?"

"I don't know."

"Most men your age know."

"I've never had a real life goal."

"Is there any major thing you plan to do in the next few months? Change, I mean."

"I plan to buy a tractor."

"And do what with it?"

"Play with the land."

"Play?"

"Yeah, play."

"You're unbelievable."

"I make some plans. I want to fence the lower meadow. I want to watch some heifers gambol over there. And I want a pond. The state will help you put in a pond. And I've been fixing up a place in the barn for a shoat. Now, I call those sure-fire plans, even for somebody like me, dilettante in all areas." I poured her cup full.

She blew in her cup to cool it. "Well," she said, "I have something to tell you. I've taken a job."

"What kind of job?"

"A job job. I don't intend to make it a career, but I want to see what it's like going to work for a while. Real work. It's a job at a printing plant on Highway 19."

"Doing what?"

"Running a press. Anything. I don't care. To be honest about it, I'm bored. You work in the mornings. Then we have lunch. Then you take long walks. Sometimes I go with you. Sometimes I don't. And when we're not doing a day that way, you're off talking to all these people you find funny and interesting. I just don't happen to think everybody is quite as entertaining as you do. I'm going to work."

"Where does that leave me?"

"At home—where you want to be."

"When do you start?"

"Monday."

I've never seen her so resolute. She said she planned to work at the printing company until she got the feel of having a job and being away and that during that time she hoped to decide exactly what she would do with her life, professionally. I gave her my blessing, though not with whole heart, and we turned out the lights and went to bed, she to sleep and me to toss.

Wednesday: Without my wholehearted blessing, my wife has found a job and gone to work it. I have lost a good and cherished daytime companion. I don't need professional help to learn my cracks. I am selfish; so, given the diary, would be any man. Let me say how the days were when the days were fine:

We always set the alarm for six because we always planned to be energetic enough to get up at six. But we always set the alarm back to seven when it rang at six. It did not bother me, the alarm going off at six, because I always went to bed intending to get up, and I always woke up intending to sleep. She and I really liked that extra hour.

We each had a little bathroom time and a little mutual, non-verbal kitchen time and then we got the kids up. The kids were a little hard to get along with at that hour, but we got them fed, and it wasn't all that hectic, and we got them dressed and I drove them to school. I started driving them to school, rather than have them take the bus, because it gave me a chance to go to town for a paper.

When I got back with the paper, she was in a better mood, as was I. We had breakfast and read funny headlines to one another: Mounds of Evidence Bared in Topless Case! Or: Ol' Man Winter Dips Icy Finger into Dixie. Hitler Was Vegetarian—Historian. And we many times ate sausage we had put through the grinder ourselves the night before. Then I would go to work. (In season, I would go trout fishing, come back for lunch, nap, and then go to work.)

While I worked in the living room, she worked in and around the house and left on errands once or twice a morning. It seemed she was always going to Mrs. Seabolt's for milk and butter, and returning with tales to tell. She has a friend lives down the road and the two of them were forever off on scouting expeditions, and spending money on pie safes we did not have room to accommodate, cupboards I did not have inclination to refinish, great oak doors that do not fit this house.

We would have lunch about one. I make a delightful bacon, lettuce and tomato sandwich, as well as no mean tuna fish. Sometimes we would have a pound of shrimp to boil and peel and dip into a light lemon and butter sauce. Always a light lunch. Once I suggested a baked potato stuffed with sour cream and caviar, and washed down with ice cold shots of vodka, but we never got around to it.

We went to bed after lunch. Sometimes we took naps.

About two-thirty, I went for a walk, most times accompanied by her. We looked for tracks, usually finding signs of rabbit, fox and yard dogs. Down the old rutted road runs beside the meadow, onto the footlog spans the creek, cut to the right where the branch makes a curve round a fine old beech. We'd check on the wood ferns and the ginger and the holly, then jump the branch and walk through a stand of hickories to a small pasture ringed with tulip poplars. About here, in cold weather, I'd pull out the small Smith Bros. cough syrup bottle, open the cap, and we would both have a hit of your basic seven-year-old, ninety-proof, Evan Williams Genuine Sour Mash. She would thrash about as if it were killing her, then accept a second short pull. Up a footpath through short needle pines to the high meadow, where we would run to and from one another, finally coming together and collapsing in the broom sedge, lying on our backs and figuring faces out of clouds.

When it rained we just sat on the front porch and looked off, like dogs do when they piss on bushes.

Back at the house, I returned to work and she prepared for dinner. Almost everything was taken care of by 4:05, when the school bus gave us back our children. The boy got on his pony in good weather and we did not see him again till dark. The girl headed west on foot to visit a friend.

Dark. Dinner. Conversation. Arguments. Unsolicited, and, for the most part, unheard parental advice. Baths. Homework. Blizzard-screen TV. Reading. And so to bed.

I loved the routine. It never got old to me.

Four-thirty, Friday: I expect the happy little press-person home any minute now, paycheck in hand, grin of independence spread wide. A quick study, she has even picked up the lingo: "The *Eagle* craps today!"

True, my occupation has landed us in more than one hard and necessary spell of parsimony, but none so serious, or lengthy, as to move a generally sane woman to money madness. "I'm going to spend the whole check on things we absolutely do not need," she said last night.

I write for magazines. I write no more nor less than one story a month. I find even that amount of production difficult, but I do it because I too like money—am not slap crazy about it, but do find a certain comfort in feeling my pocket change surround and attack the keys.

For example, last month, I had to go to Miami to do a story on the world's champion trap shooters. I do not like Miami, though my work takes me there often. To me, it lies in some awful area between infirmary and bone yard and jumping off place. Too, I found trap shooting a dull, boring sport that produces dull, boring world champions. But I did it, and two weeks ago we received in the mail a check from *Sports Illustrated* and thus had avoided impecunious times, paid the bills, and had running money for another thirty days. I call that living. It is my notion I am always exactly one idea this side of solvency. Obviously, my wife likes life more solidly footed.

She is not working just because she wants spree money, I know that. I go into this money thing only to shore my pride. I like knowing it was not entirely necessary she abandon me to these monastic days. There does not beat within me the heart of a recluse. The heart of a whiner, maybe, I'm beginning to think. Solitude eight hours a day is dangerous to the health of a gregarious man.

This has not been a week one would classify grand.

She is gone in the truck, taking her coffee with her, at seven-thirty. As she leaves, the children, who are very touchy at that hour, are just beginning to dress in front of the fire. I no longer take them to school. I no longer get a newspaper. A neighbor who likes to sleep late picks them up at eight-fifteen. By then, we have argued over breakfast. The girl likes link sausage, the boy likes patties, and on, and on, and on. For some odd and ironic reason, considering her mother's employ, the girl is down on pants this week, much prefers dresses. The boy won't wear the good jeans, prefers the kneeless look.

They are gone and I am alone. I wash the dishes and clean the kitchen and write letters. I put the letters in the mailbox, raise the red flag to attract the postman's attention, return to the house for work. Dammit, forgot about the animals. I go down to the barn, pour pails of sweet feed for the equine, break off blocks of hay, scatter laying mash for the chickens, give the two new Angoras their foul-looking pellets, return to fill the dog and cat dishes on the back porch. Then back to work. Immersed in low thought, I hear the telephone ring.

"I forgot to remind you," she says. "This is Thursday. You have to go get the milk and butter from Mrs. Seabolt."

"What time?" I say.

"About an hour ago."

"How's work?"

"Couldn't be better. How's yours?"

"Oh, not too bad."

"You'll be fine," she says, "once you establish a routine."

"So long."

"Good-by."

Into the car and out to Mrs. Seabolt's, who gives me three quart jars of snap beans canned last summer. "Something for your trouble," she says. "Coming all the way out here and all. How's that Frigidaire doing?" She pronounced it Frigi-dah-ree, with emphasis on the last two syllables. She sold it to me for twenty dollars, which came to sixty-five cents for each year of its life.

"All right," I say. "Makes a lot of noise. But freezes good."

"You have any trouble," she says, "you bring it back. I 'spect that box'll outlive me, though."

Nice woman, if I just had the time.

Home again! Home again! Peel the potatoes, wash the carrots, chop the onions, salt and pepper the roast. Roll 'em and a roll 'em and a . . . Throw 'em in the pan!

A quick BLT and back to work. No nap today. No sweet, somnambulistic noontime touchy-feely. I stay at my desk for two hours, and at the end of two hours I have written this: "Mule turd." Which has nothing to do with my subject, but a great deal to do with my mind.

Out for a solitary stroll, same old path. I am thinking, Maybe she won't like work. My sister, who is a teacher in a public school in another state, does not like work. Down here on a visit not long ago, she gave us a clear picture of the life of the only white teacher in an inner city school. "Yo' mamma," one of her charges had yelled at her, "is a skin diver fo' the Roto-Rooter!" I gave her a pep talk, and she returned to work firmly resolved to announce, "Now class, from this day forward I would like to be addressed as Mrs. McLeod. Not the honky bitch." But this has no bearing on my wife's situation. It is only what I am thinking as I am stomping through the woods.

In thick quiet, I walk along the briar patch that grows beside the branch. My steps scare up a covey of bobwhite, and all that sudden loud fluttering frightens me. For a few moments, I can hear my heart.

I am back at the house at three-thirty and I begin to split firewood. We burned all the dry wood during a solid four-day rain. Then it turned cold and the wet wood froze. Even the pine is steel-rail hard. I tap the wedge in and then slam it for all I'm worth. I am slamming away when the school bus pulls up.

"Hey, Dad," the boy yells, "Amon ride the pony down to Michael's." My children have picked up the rhythms and cadences of the local speech. "Amon" means "I'm going to . . ." The other night, after lighting a bottle rocket in the front yard, the boy hollered, "Gaw! Ju see 'at 'un?" Translation: "God! Did you see that one?"

"Dad," the girl says, reaching the woodpile, dragging her good coat in the dirt, "Ju get the water on?"

"It's on," I say.

"Good," she says. "Amon give my baby doll a bath."

I've neglected to mention the water problem. A few weeks ago, we developed a hot water leak in the shower. This was good because it kept the pipes from freezing. However, we developed a world class growth of mildew in the bathroom. So I repaired the leak, painted the walls and ceiling, went to bed with a slight feeling of accomplishment, woke up waterless. About here is where I really put the old noggin to work. I got my wife's prized electric blanket, wrapped it tight around the pipes, turned it up to High, and thawed the works.

Since then I've given the electric blanket daily employment. One morning I used it to shroud the frozen pump on the well.

Next morning, back to the pipes. For two weeks now that blanket has been everywhere but the bed.

Now it is four-thirty and I am back in the house with a load of ice wood. I go to the kitchen and tilt high the Smith Bros. cough syrup bottle, wipe my mouth on my sleeve, replace the cap, take off the cap, hit it again, replace the cap. I heartily disapprove of drinking alone before sundown, but my girl is home with me and the sun sets early here in winter.

I am fiddling with the fire when my wife comes in the door. "Ummmm," she says. "Smells good."

"Got a roast going in the kitchen."

"Wonderful. Having a hard time with the fire?"

"Yeah. Wood is frozen."

"Did you have a good day?"

"I'm adjusting."

"Well, I have some news," she says. "It seems the worst time of year is coming up for the printing company. They lay off almost everybody. No work. I'll probably lose the job in a few weeks."

"Pity," I say.

"I'll just get another job doing something else. Anyway, uh, in the meantime, I got paid today."

"I suppose you're flush as a show dog?"

"Not exactly. But it was enough to do a few things."

"Like what?"

"Like hire a baby-sitter for the whole weekend."

"What do you plan to do?"

"You mean, what do we plan to do?"

"Yeah. What do we plan to do?"

"Go down to the city, get a room in a hotel, see two plays and two movies and eat six glorious meals."

And we did and it was fine. But on Monday she returned to work, and I to make the best of things.

Amy Before They Found Her

Amy Carter, eight, and her grandmother, Lillian, seventy-eight, live in southwest Georgia, in Plains, land of the frog and the gnat, slow-moving trucks and buck haircuts and skillet-flat fields frying in the sun. Though the girl and her grandmother are the better known of the six-hundred-something permanent citizens of Plains (Jimmy, Amy's transient father, is of course best known but seldom home), they move about as inconspicuously, as unregarded, as the sound of spring plowing. The bunting hangs in the West, the speeches fall on Oregon; Amy is in school, Lillian at the pond house.

Driving down 280, Plains can be approached, seen, passed in six heartbeats, and then a hard road runs off to the left, and the red dirt road to the left of that. Miss Lillian, as she is called locally, and her pond house are on a rise to the right, deep in the piney woods. Most first-time visitors overshoot the mark, and turn round in the next-door drive of a clapboard shack, four dead cars in the chicken-tracked yard, one live gray tractor out back, an icebox on the front porch.

Turn round and go back a hundred yards.

Miss Lillian stands at the door, hair solid white, face brown and lined, smile like her son's. The house is ocher, board and batten, with a cedar shake roof and a lot of glass, and it stands naturally as the dogwoods by the flat brown pond. "Come in, come in," she says. "I have a hangover from wrestling."

She sees curiosity form on the face, and laughs.

"I love wrestling. I went last night and I'm hoarse from hollering. When Jimmy was governor, I went to the wrestling in Columbus every Wednesday night for four years. Jimmy says I probably got him two thousand votes in Muscogee County from going to wrestling. Of course I used to sit in the stands but last night they had a reserved seat in the front row and they wouldn't let me pay my way in. I had to sign autographs last night." She frowns. "And all the people I used to sit with came down to say hello. There was this one dear old man who was chewing tobacco and he had it running down both sides of his mouth and he came up and he had to hug me. Ugh."

Miss Lillian settles in an overstuffed easy chair and swings her legs over the arm. "You just ask me anything and I'll tell you the truth or nothing," she says. "I don't mind men reporters but I loathe women reporters. The only time I've been misquoted was by a woman—I won't tell you who it was—but she had me saying, 'Wallace, that stinker!' I say worse things, but I didn't say that about Mr. Wallace. . . . One thing Jimmy taught me is to just let it go and it will die down in about two weeks. And it did. Could I get you some coffee?"

Miss Lillian returns with cup and saucer and sets them on the latest issue of *Newsweek*, the cup and saucer covering part of her son's chin and nose and the headline: Carter Sweeps.

"No, the way Jimmy told me was, well, I have to go back a little bit. I had crushed my shoulder in a fall when I was in Hawaii. It was a painful thing and it still bothers me. I was in my room at the mansion in Atlanta, and Jimmy was in the rocker, beside my bed. I said, 'Jimmy, what will you do when you're not governor anymore?' I know him so well. I knew he wouldn't be content just to come back to Plains.

"He said, 'I'm going to run for President.'

"I said, 'President of what?'"

It is 10 A.M. and the bells are ringing and the classes are chang-
ing at Westside Elementary School, a one-story pale green concrete block building that sits between a cornfield and a Negro
church and is home, seven hours a day, to 530 students, 40 per
cent of whom are white, one of whom is Amy Carter, third
grader, now entering Mrs. Berda Hicks's math class, barefooted.
In the past two months, Amy has misplaced three new pairs of
tennis shoes. Miss Lillian is mildly annoyed over this. The girl
goes to school in shoes, comes home without them.

"Now," Mrs. Hicks is saying, "the first thing we're going to do
is have a little review."

The class groans. Mrs. Hicks draws a rectangle on the green
board and in the rectangle she draws fourteen squares and she
asks the class how she can show one half of fourteen and they
shout, "Shade seven." Outside the aluminum sash windows, beyond the basketball goal, a tractor works its way through the
cornfield.

The children are told to take out their pencils and to draw two
circles with horizontal lines in them to illustrate three fourths of
twelve. These are called "sets." Done right, there will be nine
lines in one circle, three in the other. Amy and five or six of her
fellow scholars finish quickly and surround Mrs. Hicks to show
her their papers. And Mrs. Hicks says, not harshly, "Sit down. Sit
down. Sit down. Sit down. You children know better than to
crowd around me." The carrot-topped daughter of James Earl
Carter walks slowly back to her desk, checked and slightly stung
by it.

Across the hall from Mrs. Hicks's math class, a tall, bearded,
stick of a man named Claude A. Frazier is fetching a bottle of oil
of clove and a Q-Tip from the closet. "Two things they need to
offer in school administration," Frazier says. "Dentistry and medi-
cal science." Frazier, the principal, dips the tip in the oil and
gently touches a small black boy's aching molar with the temporary painkiller. The boy will go to the dentist this afternoon.

Frazier resumes his seat at his desk. "One of my teachers got a
little miffed yesterday," he says. "There was a reporter here from

the Miami *Herald* and she asked the teacher when the school was integrated. When she was told, she said, 'Why did you take so long?' My teacher told her, 'No one consulted me about it.' " The school was integrated in the mid-sixties.

Here lately, Frazier has been questioned a few times about racial problems. "Vandalism around here is nonexistent," he says. "The only security we have is a windowpane. You can break any window you want and get into any room. In the last three years we've lost two baseballs and a bat. I feel like if there'd been much racial tension involved we'd of lost a little more than that, don't you?"

And as for Amy Carter, Frazier says, "She's just another student, as far as the students are concerned, and the teachers . . . She is one of our better students. She's a bright little girl. She gets along well with her classmates. She's never been a discipline problem. She ranks in the very upper part of her class. I wouldn't say that she is the very best, but she would be among them."

And as for Jimmy Carter, "There's a certain amount of excitement around here, but no more than when he was running for governor. Who would have ever thought anybody from Plains would be governor of Georgia?"

The bells are ringing. Amy has a spelling test.

Last night, Walter Cronkite was talking about Carter, and news film was being shown as Cronkite brought the country up to date. Miss Lillian yelled upstairs to Amy, "Amy, here's your daddy!"

Amy yelled from beyond her No Admittance sign, "Aw, Grandmama, I've seen him." She did not come down.

Miss Lillian is saying, "Jimmy wanted me to help him with the campaign. But I've done so much traveling. And this, you can see, look out that window there, this is the most peaceful place on earth. He finally said, 'Would you take charge of Amy?' And I said, 'Yes. That's my job. That's what I want to do.' "

Carter and his wife Rosalynn have three sons, all in their twen-

ties. He jokes that he and his wife were angry with one another
for years and years, then made up, thus: Amy.

"Amy knows the importance of her parents being away. When
they bring her by she never cries. She says, 'Grandmama, I'm so
glad to get back out here . . .' I do everything to make her happy.
My life is Amy's."

This year of the campaign is the first time Miss Lillian has had
a small child with her for any sustained period in over thirty years.
She says she loves playing mother at seventy-eight. She has always
been active. At sixty-eight, she served two years with the Peace
Corps in India. During those two years, her kin had the pond
house built for her. She has "a brick house by the hard road in
town," which she uses in the winter. And she and Amy drop by
the town house for a half hour of piano practice each afternoon
after school. "Amy's not a Paderewski," Miss Lillian says. "But
she enjoys it."

The digital clock atop the television on the hearth has just
turned 12:01. Miss Lillian and Carter's press aide in Atlanta have
warned that all interviews must terminate at noon. The word is,
Miss Lillian needs her rest. She is getting on in years. The inter-
viewer, a nap lover himself, begs leave.

"Oh," Miss Lillian says. "That is such a lie. Such a lie! The
truth is, I have to watch my favorite television program. That's
what that twelve-o'clock business is about. *The Young and the
Restless*, it's called."

Over at Westside Elementary School, they are serving soup,
milk, half a peanut butter sandwich and half a pimento cheese
sandwich. Few but Amy Carter like pimento cheese. She accepts
five halves from classmates happy to be rid of them.

Plains has been picked over too many times to be seriously
picked over again. It has five churches, a dozen stores, a railroad
track and a depot serving as Carter Campaign Headquarters and
all the ambience one would expect of a town this size.

There is no black-white problem to speak of and maybe that's
due to timidity and maybe that's due to a total acceptance of old

ways. It does have an our-nigras-are-good-nigras atmosphere. Nobody frets bussing because the only way most children get to the elementary school or the high school is by bus. Civil rights opened the school and the drugstore lunch counter to the blacks and other than that no gains can be seen. The young whites call blacks blacks and the old whites call blacks nigras or coloreds. The older, wealthier white women still speak of how hard it is to find decent help, especially since they opened the nursing home down the highway. Maids get $2.30 an hour and sometimes "aren't worth thirty cents," some say. A good maid is spoken of as "one of the cleanest nigras in Sumter County."

Miss Lillian says nigra and colored, meaning no offense. It is the way of the old. She has a maid for heavy cleaning two days a week. She does the cooking for herself and Amy. She stays by herself when Carter is in town, usually a day a week, or Rosalynn Carter, usually two days a week, and Amy goes with her parents. "I'm afraid of nothing but snakes," she says. Far as blacks go, Miss Lillian is said to have given of her time and her money and her care—she was a nurse for many years, and helped to keep her family afloat during the Depression—and has sweated much as anybody in a hot black church on funeral day.

Amy goes to the majority black public school, rather than one of the county's two private schools, both largely attended by the children of those of Carter's station, because Carter has long been an advocate of the public school system. She went to public school in Atlanta in first grade, Carter's last year as governor. "Besides," Miss Lillian says, "Jimmy's sentimental about his home. He went to school here, after all."

And though no one says it, it's a politically good shot.

And the school lets out on May 21, an early date by most of the country's school system schedules, because it gets hot as hell down here and the children grow listless and no one can think much so why waste time.

Amy spends the summer in swimming pools here and there. Her father taught her to swim when she was three. He taught her in the swimming pool of a neighbor across the street from the

governor's mansion. He tried to build a pool at the mansion, saying, "I think better at the bottom of a pool." But the Atlanta
newspapers wouldn't hear of it, said it was a waste of money, pic-
tured him ridiculously in cartoons. Carter backed off. Amy went
across the street to swim.

At five of three, Miss Lillian drives past Carter Campaign
Headquarters, Carter's Antiques, Carter's Wholesale, Carter's
Warehouse, the huge "Plains, Georgia, Home of Jimmy Carter,
Our Next President" sign and with some difficulty tries to find a
parking space outside Westside Elementary School. Miss Lillian,
a widow twenty-three years, the mother of four, the grandmother
of fourteen, is no longer a good driver. She backs her big sedan
within a hair of a pickup truck. "Look out," its driver hollers.
"Look out. Stop!" She pulls forward, stops on the grass to the
right of the gravel.

She steps out of the big dark car, a little old lady in tennis
shoes.

"Hi, Miss Lillian." It is Carolyn Anderson, a Plains woman sitting in her station wagon, waiting on her young.

"Carolyn," Miss Lillian says. "So nice to see you. Who is that
fat man over there?"

"Pardon?"

"Who is that fat man over there, one that yelled at me to stop?"

"I can't see him from here, Miss Lillian. I don't recognize his
truck."

"Well, how are you, Carolyn?"

"Oh, fine, just fine. You know, Miss Lillian, it's gotten so we
can't come downtown anymore without getting dressed up and
putting on make-up. All these news people about. Taking pictures
and movies."

"Carolyn, I know it, I know it. People say, 'What will this do
to Plains?' Well, I just want a restaurant. Just one good restaurant
is all I want. And I won't cook any meal except breakfast."

"Have they put the Secret Service men at your house, Miss
Lillian?"

"No, not yet, but one of them was just telling me—they're such nice men—that it won't be long before they'll have to have one with us. And, oh, there goes my privacy and everything. . . ."

Frazier, the principal, is out guiding children onto the big, fat yellow school busses.

"He is such a sweet man," Miss Lillian says, pointing Frazier's way. "Tuesday, I came down here to get Amy out of school to take her to Atlanta. It was ten-thirty in the morning and I told him I was sorry to have to do it. He said, 'Law, Law [Lord, Lord], Miss Lillian. Her daddy's gonna be the next President of the United States. It doesn't matter what she does.'"

Amy emerges from a side door, dirty kneed and stringy haired. "There she is," Miss Lillian says. "Barefooted as a yard dog. Child, where are your shoes?" The third grader returns to the classroom, comes back with sandals in hand.

A black man pushes a lawn mower round and round Miss Lillian's brick house in town. Inside, in the wood-paneled living room, Amy is on piano, playing "Good King Wenceslas" and "Mister Wiggle Nose" and "Camptown Races." "Play 'Echo,'" Miss Lillian says. She is sitting in a rocker by the piano.

"I'm not going to play 'Echo,'" Amy says. "I'd make a fool of myself."

Miss Lillian is driving up ahead. She is heading for her riparian retreat. I am following in another car, and Amy is at my side. She has consented to grant an interview. Interview with an eight-year-old:

"What do you think about your dad running for President?"

"All right."

"Do you think much about living in the White House?"

She shakes her head negatively.

"Well, when you think about it what do you think about it?"

"All right."

"Do you like your school?"

"Yeah."

"What do you like about it?"

"My friends. Turn left here."

"Okay."

"You don't know the way, do you?"

"Not really."

"I didn't think so. The others like you don't either."

"Oh, do you grant many interviews?"

"Do I what?"

"Do you talk to a lot of reporters?"

"No. They all want to talk to Daddy and Grandmama. Do you want to know what my favorite meal is?"

"Sure."

"A great big Coke. And fried chicken. And after, a cake with chocolate icing. A vanilla cake with chocolate icing. Do you want to know my favorite TV program?"

"Sure." I am beginning to feel stupid.

"*The Flintstones* and *The Brady Bunch*. Used to be *The Electric Company*, but no more."

"Well, tell me what exactly to you is 'all right' about your father running for President?"

"Well—here we are; turn in this driveway—what's all right about it is, well, it would be all right if he wins. Then we get to move into the White House and that's what's all right about it."

"What do your friends think about it?"

"You can stop here. They think it's all right. Now I'm going to play." She is out of the car and on to the gym set.

"Hey, Amy!" I yell after. "Do you like living with your grandmother?"

"I like living with my mamma and daddy better."

Miss Lillian and Amy rise each day at seven. Miss Lillian cooks breakfast and Amy eats at the hearth, near the broom sedge brooms and the African violets. She watches television. In the afternoons, the girl and her grandmother fish in the spring-fed pond, and more often than not catch bass, which someone else cleans for them. The girl reads in her hammock. "She is an inveterate reader," Miss Lillian says. Lately, the girl has been reading

The Clue in the Diary, Alice in Wonderland, a paperback *Partridge Family* story, and *Pets at the White House. Pets at the White House* is opened to "Mr. Jefferson's Mockingbird." Three days a week, Amy has a friend over to play with.

It's a quiet life, as they say. The kid and her grandmother are in bed at nine. Just before retiring, Miss Lillian takes one slug of bourbon.

All My Friends Are Stress-Ridden

We have just dug out from an avalanche of visitors and I am alone this morning for the first time in fifteen days. Living where we live, we are awfully popular in a cyclical sort of way. We are in demand in spring, in all but the dog days of summer, and in the few glorious days of fall. In this, the most recent case, we were covered with people in an unusual, warm, dry spell in late winter. I did not mind it, though I feel rotten from drinking too much and going too long without sleep. What I do mind, though, is that everyone I know seems unhappy, afflicted with terminal malaise, angst, melancholy, depression, whatever. They have looked into childhood to find their future, into Kubrick's future to find their past, into the present to research the core of their unhappiness, and still they have no answers. They walk around in some kind of vague pain. What the hell is wrong with everybody?

To my friend from California who stopped by en route to Maine, I said, "What are you going to do in Maine?"

He said, "Cut firewood. Sell it in the cities. Find some peace of mind."

Why does a man who has been a student for most of his life, except for the time taken out to fight a war for us, have to move across an entire continent, buy a chain saw and a truck and head for the birches to find peace of mind?

Well, he said, there is more to it than that. He does not want to have to work for anyone. He wants independence. He wants never to be humiliated. He wants, he said, what I have. And therein lies something key to our popularity.

Once more, I had to explain. I owe the bank for our land. I owe the school for the boy's trombone. My debts to my wife are immeasurable, if I choose to look at them that way. So, too, are the children's due. I do not have one boss, but many. They all live in New York, where it is thought that we who live where I live are quaint, cute and occasionally clever. We are not by any means entrenched. We live where we do so that we might know it, get some feel of it, but we did not come here figuring lasting bliss was at hand. We did not come here for peace of mind and we have not got it. I myself figure I never will. My life, and I emphasized this to my Maine-bound friend, is as malleable as the thinnest Goodyear reject. Moral: There ain't no answer. Philosophy: Too much introspection will destroy you.

Some of my friends hate their bosses, something I once did and no doubt will do again. Some have nicely worked out their employment and money situation, are comfortable, have nice houses, healthy children, yet find themselves on the brink of breakdown while picnicking. To them, I say I just don't know; whatever dark mental nag they suffer, I just don't know.

On the last day of one young man's visit, I drove him to the florist so he could purchase carnations, then to the market for fruit, then to the five-and-dime for a clean white handkerchief. He was to be inaugurated next day into the burgeoning class of transcendental meditation hopefuls.

I read that we are a nation of neurotics, and I believe it. So I'm a neurotic. Equipped with a mercurial psyche, I suffer from Walker Percy's mood swings; morning terrors, evening exaltations. But I don't color my life with it. Cope, dammit, survive. We're so inundated with psychological fadism that perfectly sane people are taking perfectly normal mental boogers seriously. These are my friends. Out of the bunch, one truly has troubles. Out of the nation, thousands are honestly afflicted—and thousands are so empathetically afflicted that you can pick a plug from among them, tell her you admire her hat, and she will perceive the remark six ways and slug you.

I hate preaching. It's just that I see so many good people buckling under their pop-psychology-filled heads. There are enough true bad-offs around, my friends. Come home for a reality check.

Trapper

Her father and grandfather farmed in the summer and trapped in the winter and when she was nine Dorothy Gooch learned the fox will run the ridges, the possum will stay to the dumps, find a henhouse and find a skunk, mink or weasel, wade the rivers and the creeks and set the traps in the slides of the beaver and the muskrat. This was the lesson of the Blue Ridge Mountains. Make do. Use a light at night and the deer will stand still before you. Learn to can, learn to pickle. Learn to clean, stretch and dry your hides and learn to do it quickly, time being money.

She was married early on, became a mother early on, a divorcee at seventeen. She moved about. She worked all night every night in textile mills and learned to drink beers at daybreak. When she was thirty-five or so, she met a man named Frank, a good provider, a heavy equipment operator, and they were married in the north Georgia valley they had grown up in; Dorothy Gooch choosing to be married in blue jeans, Frank Gooch choosing instead to buy her a $40 dress.

Frank built them a cinder block house on a gashed-out side of a mountain, just beyond a trout farm, fifteen miles north of Suches, twenty miles south of the North Carolina line, and Frank went to work cutting timber for a living. Dorothy was to stay home, be a woman, be a wife, be a mother to Frank's daughter by an earlier marriage. Her own daughter was married and gone. Dorothy Gooch went, she said, crazy. She could not stay in the house. Housework, she said, "is for maids—and ladies." Three years ago she bought six hundred steel traps and returned to the business she had learned for her father. She did well her first two seasons, earning $1,500 in one, $2,000 in the second. But this, the third, was bad.

It has not been a good winter, one learns. It looked to be a good one on November 20, the opening day of trapping season, and Dorothy Gooch was ready. The traps were rusted, the way they should be, having been left in the rain. A new trap, a well-oiled trap, assaults the senses of the fox, the bobcat, all the rest. Her four-wheel drive Bronco was tuned up and running sweet. Her father, who is seventy-two and too old to trap (and long ago stopped talking to strangers), would serve as her driver, letting her out at one point on the Toccoa River, picking her up a mile and a half downstream. They would run two hundred traps a day, ranging seventy-five miles from home, starting before light, ending in dark. Finding her catch, she would drown the beaver, the muskrat, the mink, club the possum, shoot the fox and the bobcat and the skunk. Shoot the skunk quickly before it sprays. Then run to it, pull its tail up tight as you can, spread its hind legs and it will spray on the ground. The pelt will bear no odor. "If you don't like the smell," Dorothy Gooch says, "you're in trouble." (Frank Gooch says, "Skunk don't like the smell no better than you do.")

But she took a spill on her fresh-mopped living room floor and suffered a concussion before the season was well on. The cold weather made her head hurt; her sinuses acted up. Frank Gooch stopped his wife from wading the waters. She had to be content with a few traps in the woods. There were no bobcats this year ($50 a pelt) and few red fox ($30) and fewer gray fox ($38). She was not fit to trap. She went hunting one day and killed a buck deer on the wrong land and had to give up $300 for the act. And, woe upon woes, they introduced a bill in the state legislature to outlaw steel traps. This is the fight Dorothy Gooch talks about as she sits before her fire, the mantel adorned with a symmetrical arrangement of bobcat paws.

"Those damn Humane Society ladies don't know a damn thing about what they're talkin' about. Excuse my language. Can I get you a drink?" Mrs. Gooch, an attractive woman though chain mail tough, with night black hair pulled tight to the rear and braided in one long braid down her back, moved to the kitchen for a sixteen-ounce glass. She poured an inch and a half of vodka, topped it with three inches of orange juice, topped that with an inch and a half of vodka. "I'd be willin' to bet you ever' damn one of them damn ladies got a damn fur coat in their closet. Pardon my damn language."

Mrs. Gooch said she and the other trappers were getting flak from the coon and fox hunters, who are supporting the steel-trap ban. The hunters' dogs, the well-trained blue tick or red bone or other hound, are forever getting caught in the traps. "I got one little dog out there been caught in a trap dozens of times. Now, ever' once in a while, when you're lookin' at him, he'll hobble around just for sympathy. But he ain't hurt." (For two days, it was observed that Mrs. Gooch's dog is a three-legged dog.) "The damn thing wrong with this bill is that there ain't no way in hell I can hide a two-foot-high cage. I can't trap with those damn cages. You excuse my language. I didn't have much schoolin'."

Mrs. Gooch made another drink and said, "I'm about to die bein' cooped up in this house." She headed outside and climbed in the Bronco. Driving down the serpentine road, negotiating switchback after switchback, the mountains high and bare on one side, the Toccoa River running along the other; she said, "We got no wild turkey left. The grouse is gone. You don't hear the red songbirds or the blue songbirds anymore. These animals got 'em. Ever'body in this county lost corn to the beavers last year. They dammed up the rivers and flooded a lot of the crops. You stop anywhere along here and ask any man that's got chickens if he minds me trappin' fox. He'll say, 'Hell no, woman, you go right ahead and get as many as you can.' "

She pulled into a rutted mountain pig trail, shoved the stick into four-wheel drive and said, "Come on, baby, let's roll.

"I can't afford the damn cage traps. They gettin' $15 a trap, wholesale. Right now I'm payin' $2.40 each for steel traps, $4.40 for beaver traps. Look off down yonder. You see them beaver dams. Look how that marsh grass is growin' in that bottom. Now that ain't supposed to be. That's good farmland. Was."

Now riding back to the Gooch house: "You lookee here. We got a meetin' Wednesday night of the trappers' association. Frank don't want to go but I'm gonna make him go. I'm gonna be the first woman member. Welcome to come with us."

Frank was driving, drinking a beer, and his wife sat next to him, sipping on a screwdriver. They both wore brand new jeans and jean jackets. Frank is a tall, roughhewn man, a genial outdoorsman who eats venison three times a week, year round. Frank stopped the car outside Efird's Restaurant in the mountain town of Blairsville. He and his wife went in and were shown to a pine-paneled back room where thirty trappers sat smoking and drinking coffee. Many wore overalls. Several were toothless. The Reverend Sam Henson offered a prayer:

"Dear Lord, we know that You were the first one to use the skins of little animals to clothe Adam and Eve. . . . Precious Lord, we thank Thee for putting the little animals on earth for us to trap. We pray to You, Eternal God, that You'll cause the little animals to step on the trigger of these traps, so these people can catch 'em and sell 'em and make a little money. . . . Lord, we hope too that You'll keep us in good health, 'cause You made the streams and the rivers, and we walk beside 'em and sometimes we fall in 'em. Thank you, Lord. . . ."

The moderator was Phil Nichols, a trapper and carpenter. "Now, boys, we got to organize if we're gonna fight this bill. The purpose of this meetin' is to organize the Mountain Trapper's and Landowner's Association. I was down to the Capitol the other day and me and my buddy looked kind of pitiful. The next time we go down there I want to take a busload of trappers. I don't want to go down there and find three hundred fox hunters and me by myself." Nichols proposed a ten-dollar membership fee. "I've done got us a membership card made up. There's a bobcat on one side and a beaver on t'other. I didn't go halfway. This ain't no junk."

The group voted unanimously to organize and the next order of business was the election of officers. Dorothy Gooch raised her hand and asked, "I want to know how you'uns feel about havin' a woman in this outfit?"

"Wished we had twenty more just like you," one man said.

"We wanted you or we wouldn't a invited you," said another.

Two men were nominated for president, the winner to receive the highest showing of hands. The Reverend Henson said, "Couldn't these men hide their eyes or something? I can't vote for both of 'em." The nominees covered their eyes. Mark Westmoreland, a building contractor and fur trapper, was elected president.

"I'm gonna be on 'em like a tick on a dog," Westmoreland assured the group. "I started trappin' in 1969. I got involved in it and there's nothing I love better.

"I want to tell you boys somethin'. There was a chicken farmer come up to my porch the other day and he like to cried. He said he'd lost twenty-nine hens. Night before he lost eighteen. I went over to his place and I seen his creek and I seen them chickens. Looked like somethin' had just sucked the blood out of 'em. I thought it was a weasel. I set him some traps and it turned out it was a mink. I caught that mink and that farmer like to beat that mink's head all to pieces. What I'm sayin' to you is, if this law passes, a man can't even protect his chickens."

Dorothy Gooch was elected reporter. She said she would have to learn to write and to take pictures.

On the way home, just after Frank stopped at a cornfield and spotted three deer, Dorothy Gooch said, "Frank, I'm in up to my ears now."

Frank said, "You're always in somethin' up to your ears."

They ate venison and mashed potatoes with gravy that night. Dorothy Gooch, getting out the dishes, said, "Frank, what are these things on my china cabinet?"

Frank said, "That's the bearings out of the winch to my 'dozer."

To the End

There are considerations. The boy grows older and in the growing requires more maintenance (when he is done with the boy's mouth, an orthodontist in our employ will tap us to the bone). At this moment the boy is locked in a territorial standoff with his sister, who now requires more room, more privacy. They have acquired friends, and have reached that age when friends stay over. The house grows smaller. In my naïve fashion, I continue to think we will hang on here for as long as it is good, but in the same breath I can concede that these and other trivialities will one day lead to a move.

One day, in a rare moment of serious thought, my wife and I will decide we need to move the children to a school system whose valedictorian finishes with better than a C-minus average. We'll decide I need more insurance. More insurance equals more income equals more work: Job. Job? Well, no one I know has ridden a finer gravy train longer. Slack up, lie fallow has been my message. A little period of ease doesn't hurt much, and can only enhance the journey to wherever it is one is wont to go.

Thus far in my fallow period I have been able to sing, to play guitar, to dance, drink, tell, and listen to, funny stories, walk the land, fly kites on light fishing line in the high meadow, watch the boy come whooping down the dirt road on his pony, see the girl chase, catch and let free Granny, the old hen who played out months ago. I will always like hollering when I feel like it, going to bed with my wife at noon, staying up all night reading, sleeping past noon on days of rain, buying new cowboy boots and hiring someone to break them in, growing cantaloupes that turn out big round and juicy, rather than the size of cucumbers, as they did last year, fishing and telling lies with the other liars down at C. J. Cole's dock, having friends up from the city for the best, and consistently most injurious, of all Thanksgivings. Corn bread with hot peppers and onions in it. Smoked mackerel, too. Splitting wood when the wood splits straight and easy. Cognac on cold nights and ice cold beer on hot days and women like my wife who'll go swimming with you in a trout stream so fast and cold your skin goes blue and your nips turn into marbles.

A long time ago, I found myself in a courtroom at the trial of a man who, among other things, was a heroin addict. "For God's sake," said the prosecutor, who was given to histrionics, "why in the name of anything, *anything* in this whole wide world, why did you ever get hooked up with heroin?"

"Because," the defendant said, and he stammered for words. "Because, sir, it *feels* so good."

Well, I thought then and think now, I can certainly understand that. I have not tried heroin and do not intend to, but the addict's focus is the same as mine.

I'm a grown man who can't shake seeing things with a child's selfish eyes: if it doesn't feel good, then one ought not be made to do it. Who knows? Maybe I'll be able to retain that attitude on into my own hoariness.

All of which is to say there will come a day when we no longer will receive our mail at Route Two, Wash Ryder Road. There will never be a day when we look back bitterly at the days when we did.